D0726156

This edition published by Hachette Illustrated UK,
Octopus Publishing Group,
2-4 Heron Quays
London E14 4JP

Originally published by Les Éditions du Chêne-Hachette Livre in 2002
under the title *Napoleon: L'Empereur Immortel*

ISBN: 1–84430–047–1

Library of Congress Cataloging-in-Publication Data
Gengembre, Gérard.
    [Napoléon. English]
    Napoleon: the immortal emperor / Gérard Gengembre.
      p. cm.
    ISBN 0-86565-233-3 (alk. paper)
     1. Napoleon I, Emperor of the French, 1769–1821. 2. Emperors—France—Biography. 3.
France—History—1789-1821. I. Title.

    DC203.G41513 2003
    944.05'092--dc21
    [B]

                                2003053779

Printed in Italy

NAPOLEON
HISTORY AND MYTH

With the collaboration of
Pierre-Jean Chalençon
and David Chanteranne

HACHETTE
Illustrated

Bonaparte is no longer the real Bonaparte; he is a figure of legend composed of a poet's mad musings, soldiers' accounts, and folk tales. What we see today is the Charlemagne and the Alexander of medieval epic. This fantastic hero shall remain the real person; the other portraits will vanish.

François René de Chateaubriand

Mémoires d'outre-tombe (1848)

CONTENTS

page 1: Horace Vernet,
Napoleon, 1825–1830,
pencil drawing,
private collection.

page 4: Horace Vernet,
*Napoleon I at the
Battle of Jena*.

opposite: Charles Meynier,
*Napoleon on Lobau Island
after the Battle of Essling,
23 May 1809*.

THE MARK
of the Eagle

NAPOLEON, *yet again and foreverr*—despite the long passage of time, the relative diminution of France on the world stage, and all the many social, ideological, and cultural shifts that have occurred since the Battle of Waterloo in 1815. The aura surrounding the great man glimmers even now, making him an irresistible subject of interest, fascination, and, yes, passion. Translated into immediately recognizable images and signs, Napoleon remains, in market terms, one of the most high-profile—even notorious—of all 'products.' He is a prime theme as well as a source of inspiration for literature, art, and drama, the possibilities of which never seem to abate. Transcending the limited status of historical phenomenon, Napoleon lodges, deeply embedded, within the ongoing matrix of cultural memory, thanks to his legendary and mythic dimensions, eternally adapted, remodeled, and recuperated. Co-opted by all the arts, extolled by acknowledged geniuses, theatricalized everywhere by everyone, represented in all manner of forms, Napoleon looms large in the universal imagination. His journey from one island to another, his spectacular rise and fall, his broad sweep across Europe, his immortal words, his silhouette—all have left their mark on the world. *Astre ou désastre*—brilliant star or utter disaster—Napoleon continues to be a living presence.

'Him, always him,' wrote Victor Hugo in 1829. Indeed, the whole of the 19th century basked in the light of Napoleon or shivered in his shadow. When Stendahl decided to write a book about him, he began with this admission: 'I am filled with a kind of religious sense merely by daring to write the first sentence in the history of Napoleon. He is quite simply the greatest man who has come into the world since Julius Caesar.' For many, in fact, he was their only religion. 'We have you as a god without having you as master,' again according to Hugo. In no other case has the legend of an historical figure taken on so many different colors, changing from period to period, or had his myth nourished by so many important tutelary figures. 'Alive, he failed to gain the world. Dead, he owns it,' in the words of Chateaubriand, who, more than anyone, grasped the essence of this unparalleled phenomenon. Napoleon Bonaparte forged his own legend, along the way inventing the essentials of modern propaganda. With his meteoric destiny, he gratified the Romantic movement by fulfilling its heroic dreams, its love of energy and quest for the absolute. The Napoleons cherished by the people were those who embodied their aspirations or satisfied their popular nostalgia.

A modern myth Legend, once taken up and magnified by literature and the embellish-

The First Consul, painted by Thomas Phillips in 1802, at the height of France's Consular period.

ments of oral transmission, evolves into the sublimity of myth. Napoleon pre-empts a place front and center in the pantheon of larger-than-life figures in whom humanity loves to read its own fate or symbolically dramatize the vicissitudes of its own history. Furthermore, this mythification of the Emperor coincides with his divination. From Prometheus to Jesus Christ, the Corsican General who became master of the world commands an empire of the imagination unlike any other.

This springs from his link to the French Revolution, which Napoleon salvaged, or completed, or buried, depending upon the historical, political, or ideological prism through which the record is viewed, even today. There is no denying, however, that the man who would become the new Emperor of the West did indeed emerge from the unprecedented upheaval that began in July 1789. Alexandre Dumas commented to Queen Hortense, the Emperor's stepdaughter, during a conversation at Arenenberg: 'When Napoleon, or rather Bonaparte, appeared before our fathers, madam, France was emerging not from a republic but from a revolution. In one of her attacks of political fever, she hurled herself so far ahead of other nations that she knocked the world off balance. This Bucephalus needed an Alexander, this lion an Androncles!'

In Napoleon, the century saw its origins and its guardian genius, provided it was not an evil genius. Napoleon quite simply fascinated, filling people everywhere with alarm, admiration, or hatred. He spread over the world not only a vast army, whose survivors would perpetuate his legend and nurture his cult, but also, and even more important, a new vitality. Father of a convulsive Europe, the man in the 'little hat' left no one indifferent.

The art of propaganda   Napoleon invented modern propaganda. In 1796 the young General flush with Italian victories orchestrated the chorus of praise in his own honor. Two years later the Egyptian expedition brought the glamour of Oriental exoticism; it even transformed its commander into a potential savior of a corrupt and threatened French Republic. The Directory had now found a sword, one that would permit its wielder to establish the 'dictatorship of public safety.' This came with the coup d'état of 18 Brumaire (9–10 November 1799). Beginning in 1800, the First Consul could therefore identify himself with the Savior, enriching his legend all the more. Pacifier, legislator, stabilizer, and conciliator, he became a master of laws and arts as well as arms. All that remained was for him to be crowned Emperor of the West, which took place in December 1804. From the *Bulletins de la Grande Armée* to the great battlescape paintings, from the *Imperial Catechism* to the founding of a dynasty—everything served to magnify an already complex figure, a leader idolized by most of his military, loved by the public until 1813, respected by the notables, and despised or adulated by a submissive and reconfigured Europe.

Then came 1814, the year in which the gleaming legend turned into the dark likeness of a Nero or a modern Attila the Hun. Napoleon as usurper and bloody tyrant seemed to ratify the consensus against him. Yet, the belief that no viable alternative existed, the humiliations of defeat, and the exemplary nature of his life in exile combined to re-invest the fallen hero with seductive colors. Most of all, there was that best-selling masterpiece of propaganda, *Le Mémorial de Sainte-Hélène* (1823), a journal record of everything Napoleon said during his first seventeen months on St. Helena. Quite simply, the *Mémorial* gave 19th-century youth its bible and Romanticism its ideal hero, a man marked by fate, a new Prometheus chained to his English rock in the middle of the ocean. Compiled by Marie-Joseph de Las Cases, this literary tomb, with its images of past glory, exalted dreams of conquest, and sublime visions of grandeur, proved a heady mix for younger Europeans. In contrast to the empty world around them, Napoleon evoked the exhilarating plenitude of epic endeavor, its heroic episodes forever retailed by half-pay soldiers and veterans alike.

'The most astonishing man to appear since Alexander the Great,' as Stendahl called him, kept in thrall a generation that would transpose the Imperial project into literary ambition. 'What he initiated with the sword, I shall achieve with the pen,' wrote young Balzac on the base of a portrait bust of Napoleon, purchased by the nascent writer for his attic room. To this demiurgic dimension should be added the 'rise of liberal ideas,' hailed as 'irresistible' in the *Mémorial*, where Napoleon represented himself as the messiah of the French Revolution. Now the Napoleonic myth became inscribed at the very nexus where Romanticism and liberalism converged, seen to exemplary effect in the evolution of Victor Hugo. Finally, Napoleon emerged as the bard or high priest to the nations of New Europe.

A tomb for a god The great success of the *Mémorial* in rehabilitating its author, plus the coalescence of the nostalgic and the adulatory, encouraged the July Monarchy to turn the cult of the Eagle to its own advantage. Thus in 1840 King Louis-Philippe succeeded in having the Emperor's ashes returned to France, where a state funeral would be held and the casket deposited under the great dome of the Invalides. The events proved to be a culminating moment in which the apotheosis of the legend and the consecration of the myth fused. France had now added a pilgrimage site and a patriotic monument to the pantheon of her national glories. Romanticism not only triumphed; it also became an official aesthetic that lasted for decades, contributing great numbers of art works to the Napoleonic celebration in all its variety.

The Second Empire did relatively little to exploit this enormous capital, Napoleon the Great casting too long a shadow over 'Napoleon the Tiny.' Moreover, after 1870, when Prussia defeated Napoleon III at Sedan, the dark legend itself came back to life, at least for a time. Still, the Third Republic, anxious about patriotic consensus and obsessed with revenge and the recovery of Alsace and Lorraine, found it politic to elevate Napoleon to the status of national hero. Schools extolled the victorious leader; the novelist Maurice Barrès sang the praises of Napoleonic energy; and the playwright Edmond Rostand made audiences weep over l'Aiglon, Bonaparte's ill-fated son known as the Eaglet. In 1912 Léon Bloy, succumbing to the mystique, went so far as to identify the Emperor with 'the forerunner of Him who is to come.' Meanwhile, parallel with these grandiose leaps, theatre and popular fiction, images and objects of every sort spread far and wide the legend of the 'Little Corporal.' And, from Meissonier to Detaille, painters never ceased to mine the rich Napoleonic lode.

A Napoleon for our time All these seams continued into the 20th century. The centenary of his death provided an occasion to associate Napoleon with the victory of 1918. He was also viewed as Friedrich Nietzsche's superman. Numerous historians built their careers with major works devoted to the man and his era. Writers also exploited the vein, notably those specializing in the historical novel. Surrealist artists joined in the game. Large political and ideological camps virtually defined themselves in relation to the person or the work of Napoleon, if for no other reason than to demonize him. Most of all, it was the cinema, the medium of the century, that gave the Emperor new life, both national, as in Abel Gance's peerless *Napoléon* of 1927, and international. The Emperor drew the greatest talents and assumed the features of a veritable pleiade of leading actors, in films that ranged from easy, or fanciful, entertainment to serious, patriotic works such as Vladimir Petrov's *Kutuzov*. The latter, a Stalinist picture, foregrounded the parallel between Napoleon's disastrous Russian campaign of 1812 and that of Hitler in 1941–1943.

Even today legions of people—a veritable grand army—remain fascinated by Napoleon, their entrancement reflected in the diversity of activities, creations, and products designed to satisfy a ready market. These include not only films, theatre pieces, and objects in every genre but also large auctions, countless books, reviews, collections, and even reconstructions of battles. The very tomb of the Emperor seems to radiate a thousand sparks, always adding fuel to the legend. And so the story continues to astonish. Image and example, Napoleon still hovers on the horizon of our dreams, his silhouette forever casting a long shadow onto the map of our imagination.

Inexhaustible subject of study, reference point as much obligatory as convenient, model or foil, Napoleon Bonaparte is, finally, the sum of all the memorable sites associated with his career, all that is at stake in the debate over the Revolution, over power, heroes, and great men, human will and destiny, all the components of the dream and the imagination, all the works he inspired, the objects, relics, and bibelots ultimately debased into so many fetishes. The sum but also a lesson. From the monument to the collection, from the museum to historiography, from literature to movies—everything, in final analysis, evokes the force of destiny. Napoleon reminds us that history is tragic. We have known it since the Greeks. After Austerlitz came Waterloo and then hallowed St. Helena. Immortality exacts a price. All dreams evaporate. Napoleon was indeed but a man. Herein, surely, lies his grandeur.

In 1895 Henri de Toulouse-Lautrec created this graphic
as his entry in a competition for a poster advertising
W. Milligan Sloane's *Napoleon*, a play that was about to
open in New York. An artist named Lucien Métivet won the
commission. Toulouse-Lautrec, having received nothing for
his efforts, went ahead and, on his own, printed a hundred
sheets, for distribution among friends.

In this three-quarter view, Antoine-Jean Gros
(1771–1835), an official painter among
several working for Bonaparte, produced one
of his best works, a portrait of the victorious
young General who would soon move on,
evolving into Consul and then Emperor. It
often represented Napoleon as First Consul.
The simple hat, fashioned by Poupard, was
an early version of the classic headwear now
associated with Napoleon. The model seen
here was the one the commander donned
for the Battle of Marengo (1800). Painted in
the Revolutionary Year XI (1802), the large
canvas from which this detail is excerpted
shows Napoleon, after Marengo, distributing
honorary sabers to the grenadiers of the
Consular Guard. The picture was a work of
propaganda, designed to show the soldiers'
love for the Consul, while also, and justly,
acknowledging their heroism.

NAPOLEON
on his own

IT ALL BEGINS

with propanda Talented in military matters, Bonaparte was an authentic genius when it came to propaganda. In 1796 the Italian campaign provided him with an opportunity to display his gifts as an orator and as a writer of proclamations that stick in the mind. Models of rhetoric, these utterances fixed the slogans, mobilized energies, and intensified the drama. All the Julien Sorels of Europe would endlessly read the *Bulletins de la Grande Armée*, that gospel of modern heroism. Today the reputation of Napoleon is still largely determined by the many clichés retailed throughout the first half of the 19th century, beginning with those introduced by the hero himself.

In 1799 Bonaparte understood that power within the Directory was there to be seized. He had only to position himself properly. This became the first objective. Next, he would have to hold that position. Hence the second goal, and the main reason behind the self-enrichment and the diversification of themes. Finally, it was essential to legitimate power acquired through a coup d'état—legitimate a regime or a politics of conquest and annexation. This, in turn, accounts for the third axis of Napoleonic propaganda—the control of one's own image. From the Arcola bridge to the events of Brumaire, from the position of First Consul to the coronation of 1804, from Imperial icon to military god, Napoleon evinced a magisterial command of how he was portrayed to the world. The representation of power and its master would never be the same again.

left: The energy of the adolescent Napoleone Buonaparte can be sensed even in this profile view, the first known portrait of the subject, executed in 1785 by a fellow student at the military school in Brienne.

opposite: Louis Lafitte, *Preparatory Study for a Portrait of Napoleon Bonaparte*, 1794. Long before the rash of representations linked to the Italian and Egyptian campaigns, followed by the Brumaire coup d'état, this drawing provides a rare frontal view of the young General's face.

THE SWORD
of the Revolution

The young Lieutenant from Corsica with an unpronounceable name did not truly enter history until September 1793 at the siege of Toulon, where as an artillery commander he performed so impressively that by December he had been elevated to the rank of Brigadier General. It helped that he also enjoyed the favor of Robespierre, a consequence of his relationship with Augustin de Robespierre, the Incorruptible's brother. No one, however, foresaw what an extraordinary epic Bonaparte would make of his life. His birth, his childhood, his military-school adolescence, his Corsican adventures, the vagaries of the Bonaparte family's involvement with Pascal Paoli—all would undergo numerous embellishments designed to make them consistent with the legend. However, there is nothing in this background to mark young Bonaparte as exceptional. Indeed, after Thermidor (27 July 1794), which saw the end of Robespierre and the Great Terror, he became a Jacobin General without employment. As a Robespierrist, he even spent time in jail, before setting out, with sallow skin and filthy hair, to pound the pavement in search of a commission. Nothing more was written about him, until *La Prise de Toulon*, a play about the liberation of Toulon, brought to the fore a certain heroic gunner. It was Bonaparte himself, who, at loose ends, took to composing fiction. However, luck, or more likely historical circumstance, would soon change everything. The Directory (1795–1799), as the new French government was called, desperately needed a sword capable of repulsing the royalist threat. With his famous 'whiff of grapeshot'—a cannonade fired off on 5 October 1795 (Vendémiaire)—twenty-five-year-old Bonaparte saved the day, for the government at least if not for the Republic or France. 'General Vendémiaire' could at last see a future opening before him. He also made implacable enemies among the Counter-Revolutionists, as well as some extremely useful connections. Marriage (to Josephine de Beauharnais in 1796), support, money, commissions— suddenly the young commander found himself head of

the Army of Italy. The legend now commenced, orchestrated by the beneficiary himself, who thereafter would give it his full attention. In ten weeks and ten battles, he led his troops to Milan, never failing to envelop every glorious episode in a halo of flattering propaganda. From the Arcola bridge to the Rivoli plain, the General with the eagle profile, burning eyes, and lionine mane left his mark and projected both his image and his style. His proclamations snapped like a flag blowing in the wind. If he did not write them himself, the newspapers he established for the purpose got the word out. To generate enthusiasm, he exploited every rhetorical device. The image of the Eagle had already become established. The 'Little Corporal,' as he was known after the Battle of Lodi on 10 May 1796, cultivated his popularity and prepared his triumphal return to the French capital.

From Milan to the Pyramids The next step was to become the great man of the Republic, not just one of the victorious generals. The image of Bonaparte appeared everywhere, even on bottles of

opposite: In this pen-and-ink sketch Antoine-Jean Gros saw the face of the young General as a cold, almost emaciated masque. Gros had joined an important cadre of artists whose mission was to record the thin, sallow visage framed by long hair. Most of them produced pure invention. Only Gros, Appiani, and Cossa enjoyed direct access to the hero.

left: An artist's rare reconstruction of the English siege of Toulon, which Bonaparte helped to break on 19 December 1793 by virtue of his clever gunnery. The victory made him a Brigadier General and placed his name before the public, just as his own *Souper de Beaucaire* had done in July 1793. In this political dialogue the ambitious young officer had attempted to expose the strategic weakness of the counter-revolutionaries in the Midi.

below: Jules Lecomte de Noüy, *Souper de Beaucaire*. When exhibited at the Salon of 1795, this painting had a label quoting from Bonaparte's eponymous text: 'Believe me, he said, there will come a man who will unite within himself all the nation's hopes, and then . . . .' Already the legend was underway.

perfume. Poets and playwrights alike sang his praise, notably in *The Bridge at Lodi*, a play with music by Étienne-Nicolas Méhul that opened in Paris on 15 December 1797. No one at the time could have known that on the very evening of the Lodi victory Bonaparte had conceived his 'ambition to achieve the great things which until then had occupied his mind like a dream,' as he would confess to Montholon on St. Helena. The peace-maker was applauded from every side. Admitted to the prestigious Institut de France, he flattered the intellectuals, praised the men of the Enlightenment, and set his eyes on other horizons. There he saw Egypt. To the Italian glories he would add the lustre of the Orient. Whatever the reasons for the Egyptian venture—a Directory prepared to rid Paris of an ambitious and popular General, eagerness to thwart England by attacking its interests in the Mediterranean, the Oriental dream of a Bonaparte afraid of becoming lost in inaction, an imperious need to accomplish something grand—it remains one of the truly fabulous extravagances of Napoleonic history. Born of a chimera, the Egyptian affair looms large in the legend because of the fascination exercised by the land of the pharaohs and the great flood of images it generated. Bonaparte on the back of a camel, the Rosetta Stone, marches across the desert, the exotic colors, the uniforms of the Mameluks—a sumptuous album that history invites us to leaf through. From the Po Valley to the banks of the Nile—no other French general had ever traversed so much geography. The Eagle flew every-where, taking with him the conquering Revolution, reinforced by the Enlightenment. 'Italicus' had triumphed. It was the grand tour of 'Aegyptiacus,' however couched in a bed of lies. Along with the military expedition went a scientific mission. A carefully controlled press, the symbolism of the Pyramids (even if it is not certain that Bonaparte ever pronounced on the spot the famous line 'from the top of the pyramids, forty centuries contemplate you'), the co-option of culture for military purposes,

the return to Cairo following the defeat at Saint-Jean-d'Acre—everything conspired to limn the profile of the new Scipio. Never mind that Bonaparte had to evacuate the Holy Land; he simply converted defeat into a triumph of propaganda. In 1804 Antoine-Jean Gros, future Baron of the Empire, exhibited his *Pesthouse at Jaffa*, a monumental painting that deftly assimilated Bonaparte into the legend of miracle-working kings, the better to help the world forget his abandonment of the sick and the massacre of prisoners. In this mendacious picture, Gros perfected the art of manipulation and gorged the legend. Meanwhile, Bonaparte had succeeded in extricating himself from the Egyptian trap. Several plays celebrated his return to Paris, reflecting a popularity that would only grow and become ever more embellished. Fortunately, the arrival back in France, on 9 October 1799, had been preceded by news of the land victory at Aboukir, once more an aid to those willing to forget, this time the destruction of the Mediterranean fleet. The conqueror was now ready to assume his new role—as savior of the Republic.

Napoleon: The Immortal Emperor

overleaf, pages 22–23: Carle Vernet (attributed), *The Battle of the Lodi Bridge*, c. 1808. Here Vernet, a leading specialist in the depiction of battle scenes, dealt with another legendary victory (10 May 1796). Because of his courage, General Bonaparte won the respect of his troops, who, out of affection, nicknamed him the 'Little Corporal.'

left: Carle Vernet, *The Battle of Rivoli, 14 January 1797*, c. 1808. Other than Arcola, the most often painted of the Italian episodes is the Battle of Rivoli, which turned into a strategic triumph for Bonaparte, commander of the Army of Italy. Later, the artist Félix Philippoteaux would treat the subject in a totally different manner (page 129).

above: Lethière (Guillaume Guillon), *Bonaparte Dictating the Peace of Loeben*, Salon 1806. The Italian campaign would conclude with peace negotiations signed at Loeben on 18 April 1797, when the victorious General dictated his conditions, later ratified by the Treaty of Campoformio signed on 17 October. Lethière, in his reconstruction of the scene, dramatized the diplomatic coup achieved by the young commander, who would soon depart for Egypt.

below: André Dutertre, *Bonaparte*, 1798. It was on board the *Orient*, sailing for Egypt, that Dutertre drew this profile portrait for use in a medallion. The subject still had the long, flowing hair made famous at Arcola. The heat of Africa forced him to have the locks shorn. By the time he returned to France, the Little Corporal once again sported tresses falling over his ears, neck, and brow.

25

The Sword of the Revolution

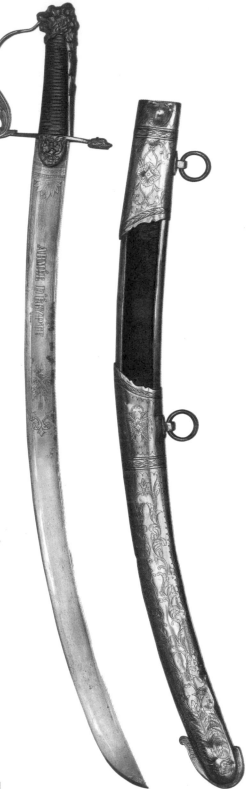

opposite: Guillaume-François Colson, *The Entrance of General Bonaparte into Alexandria, 3 July 1798*, Salon 1812. Realized well after the event, Colson's painting gave General Bonaparte the features of Napoleon, as well as the pose of a sovereign intent upon protecting the population he had conquered.

right: The saber worn by the commander at the Tuileries for the coup d'état of 18–19 Brumaire (9–10 November 1799) had engraved on its blade 'the Army of Egypt.' In this way Bonaparte established a link between the army he had left (or abandoned, as Bernadotte put it) in Cairo and France, all of which invested the saber with considerable symbolic import.

left: François-André Vincent, *The Battle of the Pyramids, 21 July 1798*, commissioned in 1800. Here the artist focused on a band of Mameluks charging dangerously close to Bonaparte, the latter mounted proudly on his horse, one arm raised in the sort of commanding gesture so often depicted in painting. The French infantry, in square formation, fires point-blank at the rapidly advancing cavalry. Later the subject would be revisited by Louis-François Lejeune.

below: Nicolas-Toussaint Charlet, *Bonaparte with His Staff in Cairo*, watercolor with gouache, private collection. While in the Middle East, Bonaparte may have mounted a camel, as later shown in paintings by Raffet and then Gérôme. More often, however, he rode a horse or walked during his journey across the desert.

above: Louis-François Lejeune, *The Battle of Aboukir*, 1799. On 15 July 1799 General Bonaparte led his troops in a land victory over an Ottoman army dispatched under the protection of the English. Lejeune, who served as an aide-de-camp to General Berthier from 1798 to 1812, made sketches of all the battles in which he took part.

opposite: Antoine-Jean Gros, *Bonaparte at the Pesthouse of Jaffa, 11 March 1799,* Salon 1804, Louvre. In this dramatic canvas Gros 'redeemed' what had been an atrocious episode, doing so in response to the real story reported by the English. The sick, rather than comforted with a healing touch, had in fact been abandoned, perhaps even force-fed on opium. Gros,

dedicated to the Bonaparte legend, magnified a leader who, like the miracle-working kings of old, touches the scrofula with a ungloved hand. Given the Holy Land setting, few would have missed the intended identification with the miracles of Christ. By contrast, Dr. Desgenettes, immediately behind the intrepid hero, covers his face so as not to breathe the foul air. The painting contributed to the divinization of the master.

overleaf, pages 32–33: The Egyptian campaign re-ignited the Egyptomania that had been underway throughout the 18th century. In 1802 Dominique-Vivant Denon, a member of the French expedition to the Middle East, was appointed director of the

Central Museum of the Arts (Louvre). While launching the Egyptian style in the decorative arts, Denon helped associate the future Emperor with Egyptianized design. *Reading from top to bottom and from left to right:* the bed of Eugène de Beauharnais, Napoleon's stepson (Musée de Malmaison); the Emperor's Egyptian chocolate service in blue-ground Sèvres porcelain decorated with hieroglyphics, Egyptian views, and, on the saucer, the image of a sheik painted by Pierre-Jean de Béranger (1810; Louvre); Egyptianized writing case, one of the first works inspired by the Egyptian campaign (Musée, Sèvres); fireplace fender ornamented with a patinated bronze sphinx, attributed to Claude Galle (Musée de Malmaison).

THE SAVIOR
of the Republic

In October 1798 Bonaparte made a triumphal return from the Middle East, applauded all the way from Fréjus to Paris. The new Aeneas reached the shores promised by the gods. Already the press had spread the word about the Egyptian exploits and the exemplary performance of a leader dedicated to the well-being of humanity. Here was the sword the Brumaire conspirators had been longing for. Their greater goal: a solid Constitution, strong power, and social stability, the better to guarantee the basic achievements of the Revolution. In response, Bonaparte made numerous pledges; indeed, he would take charge of the affair. Still, the coup d'état of 18 Brumaire almost misfired. No matter, Bonaparte quickly recovered, boldly commanding his grenadiers: 'Follow me, I am the god of the day.' Right off, politics evolved into legend. A dagger-wielding grenadier, eager to save his General, managed to slit the sleeve of the great man's uniform. This *faux* attack became the real thing, once the official version of the episode reached the world, through a descriptive engraving. The new Caesar had escaped Brutus and his blade.

right: François Bouchot, *Bonaparte at Saint-Cloud on 18 Brumaire*, c. 1848. The coup d'état of 18 Brumaire, a founding political event, generated a plenitude of iconography. Bouchot's painting, commissioned by King Louis-Philippe for the Historical Museum at Versailles, made its debut at the Salon of 1849, the year in which the Emperor's remains were returned to France. The scene focuses on the moment when Bonaparte, with his grenadiers, has just entered the Council of Five Hundred. Encircled, crowded about, and abused by the indignant deputies, the young General stands firm, while his soldiers invade the tribune where Lucien Bonaparte presides. No dagger is to be seen, and only by the pallor of his face does the hero betray a *frisson* of emotion, despite the vehement protestations on every side. With his arms folded over his chest, a tightly furled tricolore scarf looped about his neck, and clad in the uniform he wore at Arcola and the Pyramids, the General seen here has little to do with reality. In fact, Bonaparte bloodied his own countenance, clawing it with his nails in a fit of rage.

LA FRANCE AVANT LE 18 BRUMAIRE DE L'AN VIII.
Éplorée, dénuée de tout, entraînée par le Desespoir et la Discorde, elle est ranimée par l'Esperance et remise par Bonaparte entre les mains de la Paix. Le Tems trace cet heureux Jour dans les Fastes de l'Histoire.

Named First Consul on 12 December 1799, the savior of the Republic had all the more reason to cultivate and perfect his image. Now Bonaparte played the triumphant republican, while at the same time orchestrating the ritual show of power and surrounding himself with a freshly instituted Consular Guard. The bayonets of Saint-Cloud had indeed ushered in a new order. The master reveled in the myth of the savior. The very morning after the coup d'état, he proclaimed anew the principles of 1789 and forecast a radiant future: 'Frenchmen, the Republic, reaffirmed and restored to its place in Europe at the rank she should never have lost, will see the realization of all the hopes of her citizens and the attainment of her glorious destinies. Join with us and take the oath to remain faithful to the Republic, one and indivisible, founded upon equality, liberty, and the representative system.'

Much later, on St. Helena, Napoleon would offer a different interpretation of 18 Brumaire, an event destined to have profound consequences for the history of France. He merely cited what had been the overriding factor, the general concern about the risks of diminished power: '[France] seemed to want a

man who could save her. This protective genie, a populous nation always has him in her midst, but sometimes he is slow to appear. In fact, it is not enough for him to exist; he must be known; he must know himself. But once this eagerly awaited savior suddenly signals his existence, the national instinct recognizes and summons him. Obstacles slip away before him, and the whole of a great people, falling in behind him, appears to say: "This is the one!"' It would be hard to imagine a better analysis of the very principles of Bonapartism, or, more generally, the myth of the savior. Resurrected in France several times thereafter, all the way to Pétain and de Gaulle, the myth is that of a genius delivered by historical circumstance to a country drowning in chaos, and prepared to rally around a hero by finding common ground in traditional values. But only in the rhetoric of the Emperor would Bonaparte discover his true measure. Very quickly a popular version of the message came to the fore through a song: 'French friends, fear no more! / This day brings our happiness / Reason more than arms / Will make the people victorious / We will again see abundance / Above all there will be peace.' On 22 Brumaire Paris saw the first performance *Les Mariniers de Saint-Cloud*, a stage production celebrating the joy of a France delivered from her exploiters. A plebiscite would ratify the reconfigured Republic.

The apotheosis of Marengo France wanted a king born out of the Revolution. Her deep longing would be satisfied, but not from the ranks of the remaining Jacobins, or from the restive counter-revolutionaries in Western France, or yet from the militant royalists. Meanwhile, the nation had to be secured against its enemies, who were again on the march. Hence the second Italian campaign, undertaken in April–June 1800. It would enrich the Napoleonic legend with one of its most impressive pictorial representations. Painted by Jacques-Louis David in 1801, *Bonaparte Crossing the Great St. Bernard* immortalized its subject

above: Anonymous, *Bonaparte as the Savior of France*. The Brumaire coup d'état was soon appropriated by the Bonaparte legend. The official version of the event, widely parroted by the press, wormed its way into numerous engravings, prints, aquatints, etc. Bonaparte thereafter assumed the role of savior, as shown in the anonymous engraving reproduced here.

opposite: Courtin, *The Morning of 18 Brumaire*, lithograph. The preparations for the coup d'état were also depicted, with the figure of the new master thoroughly idealized. In Courtin's lithograph Bonaparte is shown departing for Saint-Cloud.

as the successor to Hannibal and Charlemagne. Almost a half-century later Paul Delaroche would demystify the episode by portraying a rather triste General dressed in gray and riding a mule led by a guide. The crossing may indeed have been spectacular, but there was nothing exceptional about traveling over the High Alps. Never mind, by actively collaborating with David, the Consul created a major icon, and he intended it to be seen. A summary document of the Napoleonic epic, the picture also

choice. Further, he could at last take over the army. freed as he was of potential rivals, thanks to the deaths of numerous generals since 1797, among them Hoche, Joubert, Championnet, and now Desaix and Kléber. Bernadotte, Brune, Augereau, Masséna, and Jourdan had rejoined the ranks. When the time came, they would be named marshals. That left Pichegru, who plotted with the royalists, and Moreau, who would win the decisive victory at Hohenlinden. Ardently courted by the rich, Bonaparte, the

co-opted royalist tradition, that of the equestrian portrait dating back to Titian's famous image of Emperor Charles V and thereafter reserved to sovereigns. As for the crossing theme, it would be taken up again in 1801, this time by Taunay, and once more by Charles Thévenin in 1805.

Marengo, 14 June 1800. The site lingers in the mind as considerably more than a dreary plain, which initially the Austrians took. Bonaparte then recaptured it, albeit for good only after the arrival of troops led by General Desaix. A battle lost but finally won, even if it cost Desaix his life. Precisely who deserved credit for Marengo became the subject of heated debate, all the way to 1806, when a third draft of the official account appeared, giving full recognition to the First Consul. Never mind again, a France bled white could once more taste victory (even though on the very day of Marengo General Kléber had been assassinated in Cairo). Bonaparte, official savior of the Republic, was now the nation's

providential man, had come into his own and could loftily reject the offers of Louis XVIII, who was convinced that the Consulate would be no more than a transition to a restored monarchy. At Marengo, an event painted by Lejeune for the Salon of 1801, Bonaparte planted his regime for sure and realized the most political of his victories. As if to symbolize this deep rootedness, Josephine had a cedar added to the park at Malmaison. Everything centered upon Marengo, which the English understood only too well. Indeed, it explains their determined effort to bring down both Consular and Imperial France.

Meanwhile, however, the proud and relieved French turned the 14th of July (Bastille Day) 1800 into a veritable apotheosis of their conquering General, even after all the fireworks that had greeted his return to Paris on the 2nd of the month. The 19th century could now begin, a bit ahead of schedule. The new Hannibal would evolve into the new Washington.

PROCLAMATION

DU GÉNÉRAL EN CHEF

BONAPARTE.

Le 19 Brumaire, onze heures du soir.

A mon retour à Paris, j'ai trouvé la division dans toutes les Autorités, et l'accord établi sur cette seule vérité, que la Constitution était à moitié détruite et ne pouvait sauver la liberté.

Tous les partis sont venus à moi, m'ont confié leurs desseins, dévoilé leurs secrets, et m'ont demandé mon appui : j'ai refusé d'être l'homme d'un parti.

Le Conseil des Anciens m'a appelé ; j'ai répondu à son appel. Un plan de restauration générale avait été concerté par des hommes en qui la nation est accoutumée à voir des défenseurs de la liberté, de l'égalité, de la propriété : ce plan demandait un examen calme, libre, exempt de toute influence et de toute crainte. En conséquence, le Conseil des Anciens a résolu la translation du Corps législatif à Saint-Cloud ; il m'a chargé de la disposition de la force nécessaire à son indépendance. J'ai cru devoir à mes concitoyens, aux soldats périssant dans nos armées, à la gloire nationale acquise au prix de leur sang, d'accepter le commandement.

Les Conseils se rassemblent à Saint-Cloud ; les troupes républicaines garantissent la sûreté au dehors. Mais des assassins établissent la terreur au dedans ; plusieurs Députés du Conseil des Cinq-cents, armés de stylets et d'armes à feu, font circuler tout autour d'eux des menaces de mort.

Les plans qui devaient être développés, sont resserrés, la majorité désorganisée, les Orateurs les plus intrépides déconcertés, et l'inutilité de toute proposition sage évidente.

Je porte mon indignation et ma douleur au Conseil des Anciens ; je lui demande d'assurer l'exécution de ses généreux desseins ; je lui représente les maux de la Patrie qui les lui ont fait concevoir : il s'unit à moi par de nouveaux témoignages de sa constante volonté.

Je me présente au Conseil des Cinq-cents ; seul, sans armes, la tête découverte, tel que les Anciens m'avaient reçu et applaudi ; je venais rappeler à la majorité ses volontés et l'assurer de son pouvoir.

Les stylets qui menaçaient les Députés, sont aussitôt levés sur leur libérateur ; vingt assassins se précipitent sur moi et cherchent ma poitrine : les Grenadiers du Corps législatif, que j'avais laissés à la porte de la salle, accourent, se mettent entre les assassins et moi. L'un de ces braves Grenadiers (Thomé) est frappé d'un coup de stylet dont ses habits sont percés. Ils m'enlèvent.

Au même moment, les cris de *hors la loi* se font entendre contre le défenseur *de la loi*. C'était le cri farouche des assassins, contre la force destinée à les réprimer.

Ils se pressent autour du président, la menace à la bouche, les armes à la main ; ils lui ordonnent de prononcer le hors la loi : l'on m'avertit ; je donne ordre de l'arracher à leur fureur, et six Grenadiers du Corps législatif s'en emparent. Aussitôt après, des Grenadiers du Corps législatif entrent au pas de charge dans la salle, et la font évacuer.

Les factieux intimidés se dispersent et s'éloignent. La majorité, soustraite à leurs coups, rentre librement et paisiblement dans la salle de ses séances, entend les propositions qui devaient lui être faites pour le salut public, délibère, et prépare la résolution salutaire qui doit devenir la loi nouvelle et provisoire de la République.

Français, vous reconnaîtrez sans doute, à cette conduite, le zèle d'un soldat de la liberté, d'un citoyen dévoué à la République. Les idées conservatrices, tutélaires, libérales, sont rentrées dans leurs droits par la dispersion des factieux qui opprimaient les Conseils, et qui, pour être devenus les plus odieux des hommes, n'ont pas cessé d'être les plus méprisables.

Signé BONAPARTE.

Pour copie conforme : ALEX. BERTHIER.

A PARIS, DE L'IMPRIMERIE DE LA RÉPUBLIQUE. Brumaire an VIII.

above: Auguste Couder, *Installation of the
Council of State at the Petit-Luxembourg Palace
on 25 December 1799.* c. 1835. Here the artist
portrayed the First Consul, flanked by
Cambacérès and Lebrun, both of them relegated
to secondary roles, receiving the oath of loyalty
from the presidents of the five sections of the
Council of State.

opposite: In the proclamation of 19 Brumaire,
the account offered of the events was unalloyed
propaganda; yet, once published, it became the
founding principle of Bonapartism: the
providential man who stood above all parties.

right and overleaf, pages 40–41: Jacques-Louis David, *Bonaparte Crossing the Great St. Bernard*, 1801, Versailles. After Arcola, the most glorified of the Consular exploits was the Battle of Marengo (14 June 1800). Among the many it enraptured was David, who immediately set about to deify the man of Brumaire by painting *Bonaparte Crossing the Great St. Bernard*. It evokes an impetuous hero astride a fiery charger as he negotiates the High Alps en route to Italy. Even as the terrified horse rears up on its hind legs at the edge of a precipice, the rider retains his Olympian calm, all the while pointing majestically at the horizon beyond a grandiose, snow-covered mountainscape. Carved into the rocks: Hannibal, Charlemagne, and Bonaparte. The canvas reflects the First Consul's expressed desire to be seen as 'calm on a spirited horse.' David completed the canvas in four months, from September 1800 to January 1801, reversing the traditions of allegory and transforming a real, living person into a timeless hero.

opposite: Paul Delaroche, *Bonaparte Crossing the Great St. Bernard*, 1848. Delaroche, in his version of the St. Bernard scene, painted almost a half-century after David's, deconstructed the legend point by point, taking his cue probably from the account given by Adolphe Thiers in his *History of the Consulate and Empire* (1840–1855). Commissioned by the Earl of Onslow, Delaroche moved closer to reality than anything attempted by David in his masterpiece. The great man did in fact ride a mule across the St. Bernard. At one point he just missed being pitched into the abyss when the poor beast lost its footing

above: Charles Thévenin, *Bonaparte Crossing the Great St. Bernard*, Salon 1806. Also commissioned by Bonaparte, Thévenin painted an accurate description of the site but placed the First Consul at the center of things. There, along with his staff, he stands on his own two feet pointing out the pass the troops were expected to negotiate on their way to Italy.

A WASHINGTON
for the French

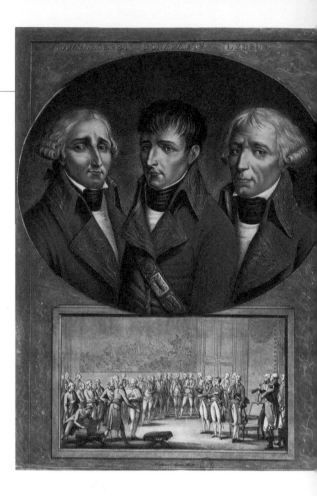

The year 1800, a time of great happiness at Malmaison. Purchased in 1799 by Josephine and fitted out by Percier and Fontaine, the château on the northern outskirts of Paris would, apart from the Tuileries, be the principal residence of the Bonapartes until the autumn of 1802, when the First Consul moved into the Château de Saint-Cloud. A place of intense work, Malmaison was also host to many pleasures and pranks. Dinners, theatre, garden parties, mock jousts, jokes, and games—all fairly burgeoned at Malmaison, thanks to the youth of the society there and the genial spirit and unbuttoned, bourgeois style favored by the reigning couple of new France. Soon, however, etiquette would replace this relaxed atmosphere, once the Bonaparte Consulate came into being 'for life' (2 August 1802), before metamorphozing two years later into the Empire (proclaimed on 18 May 1804). Now simplicity and laughter would give way to the formal requirements of court life.

All the while, Bonaparte busied himself with restructuring the institutional life of France, eliminating political opposition, and negotiating the peace. A coherent fiscal and monetary system, administrative reorganization, the return of émigrés proscribed since the Revolution, pacification of the western provinces, anti-Jacobin repression, a press kept in check, the Civil Code, the Concordat—all flowed unabated from the new master. The monarchization of the Republic gradually evolved into the dictatorship of Bonaparte and the Empire. For the moment, however, the Consul played the role of pacifier, stabilizer, and guarantor of the Revolution and its achievements, even as he rebuilt bridges to the

opposite: Jean-Baptiste Greuze, *Napoleon as First Consul.* c. 1802. The aged Greuze, a relic of the 18th century's Rousseaueque love of sentiment, produced an odd, rather feminized portrait.

above: Pierre-Michel Alix, *The Three Consuls*, c. 1801. In this group portrait, based upon a work by Vengorpe (or Vangorp), the artist gave Bonaparte a sallow, even sickly appearance.

ancien régime, which, however, he in no way restored. Actually, one might call it a government of the center, quite in keeping with the majority.

The Consul When he took over the Consulate, Bonaparte was still the General with hair as long as a spaniel's ears and a blue morning coat worn over white, close fitting breeches. Thin, high-strung, sallow, he still looked like the ambitious Corsican who had led the Army of Italy in 1796. Now, however, the face would grow fuller and the hair shorter, while the blue morning coat would give way to the crimson Consular frockcoat, a sash of white silk around the waist, or sometimes the green uniform of the horse guard (on ordinary days), or yet the blue uniform of the grenadiers (reception days or Sunday). Iconography divided into several types, one of them immortalized by Jean-Baptiste Isabey in his *Bonaparte at Malmaison.* Here, for the first time, the subject is portrayed with one hand slipped into his vest, henceforth an iconic pose universally known from countless repetitions.

Gros established a second type in his 1802 portrait of the First Consul, where the Bonaparte of

1796 is still perceptible despite the clear emphasis upon the authority of the man. In 1804 twenty-four-year-old Jean-Auguste-Dominique Ingres imbued his Bonaparte, now Emperor, with majestic serenity. François Gérard softened the features even more when he dressed Bonaparte in a cavalry uniform and set him upon a horse. Louis-Léopold Boilly, on the other hand, presents us with a Bonaparte who seems melancholic, almost sickly. Jean-Baptiste Greuze, by this time an elderly relic of the pre-Revolutionary period, managed to feminize his Consul, endowing him with sad eyes, a languid posture, and scant resemblance to the virile Greco-Roman model.

Bonaparte knew how to enjoy himself, relaxing with friends and having a good laugh, but he could also give way to terrifying fits of anger. More than anything, however, he liked to lose himself in hard work, a fact he wanted the world to know. The legend would therefore consecrate him a superman of power. In reality, Bonaparte became the first 'managerial' head of state, as Thierry Lentz so justly put it. Adept at utilizing experts, he possessed a genius for synthesis, a faculty which propaganda would translate into omniscience and omnipotence. True enough, he accomplished an enormous amount of work, thanks to inexhaustible energy and a resolute sense of power. Yet there is no denying that the passive side of his rule, such as the reinstitution of slavery, the inferior status of women, and the punitive labor policy, tarnished the active side, which, from the Bank of France to the Legion of Honor, rebuilt France solidly upon the foundation of the Revolution.

right: The original edition of the Code Civil, created by the First Consul (turned Consul for Life on 2 August 1802) at the same time that he functioned as the god of both war and peace.

opposite: Antoine-Jean Gros, *Bonaparte, First Consul*, 1802, private collection. Gros was the first artist to paint an official portrait of the Consul. Commissioned by Bonaparte, it would serve as a model for other artists favored by the Consulate.

above: Jean-Auguste-Dominique Ingres, *Bonaparte as Consul*, 1802. Also commissioned by the subject, twenty-two-year-old Ingres portrayed the master as a slight, intense young man with an inward, abstract look, providing a forecast of his image of the Emperor enthroned like Zeus (page 67). The official portraits all present the Consul standing and contrappostoed in a way traditional for images of a sovereign. Usually the great man points with his right hand to a list of his achievements, treaties, and important acts. The color of the clothes—crimson—had long been identified with power.

Towards the Empire Made Consul for life on 2
August 1802, following a plebiscite, Napoleon
Bonaparte (the first name made its official entry by
way of the plebiscite), gathered up all the reins of
power in his own hands and gained control of the
various parts of the state. Already his profile could be
seen on every piece of money. A colossal statue of
Charlemagne was erected in the Place Vendôme and
the Central Museum of the Republic—the Louvre—
renamed the Musée Napoléon in 1803, as if to
anticipate the name of the Emperor. England, which
had renewed hostilities, was denounced, and by

executing the Duc d'Enghien (20 March 1804), the
Consul for Life drew in blood-soaked lines the
impassable frontier between him and the Bourbons.

Fouché and others urged that the Empire be
proclaimed, so as 'to achieve his work by rendering it
immortal like his glory.' A Mass was said, the New
Constitution issued, and a new plebiscite conducted.
The *Sacre* or coronation was nigh .

In November 1800 Louis de Fontanes had
published a hagiographic pamphlet, comparing
Bonaparte, Caesar, Monck, and Cromwell. His purpose
was to establish a bridge between ancient Rome, the

below: Jean-Baptiste Isabey, *Bonaparte at Malmaison*, 1802. Here, for the first time, the Consul is shown in an environment of bourgeois simplicity, wearing the uniform of a grenadier and the little hat he made famous. Another canonic feature is the flexed arm with its hand slipped into the vest

left: Mathieu Ignace van Bree, *Entrance into Antwerp on 18 July 1803*, c. 1804. For the Consul to be properly represented, it was also essential that his movements be endowed with high symbolic import, as in this painting by a Flemish artist.

English Revolution, and the new French order. However, a more illuminating reference was the one made to George Washington, the General who defeated the English in the American Revolution and then went on to be elected President of an entirely new democracy. A seductive parallel indeed. 'Having gained power, one might have wished that I had been a Washington, but I could only have been a crowned Washington,' Napoleon admitted in the *Mémorial de Sainte-Hélène*, which perfectly defines what the future Emperor wanted in the way of a new monarchy. And the prototype he looked to was Charlemagne.

above: Pierre-Joseph Petit, *Château de Malmaison*, c. 1806. Malmaison, on the northern outskirts of Paris, was a key image in Napoleonic iconography.

opposite: Pierre-Paul Prud'hon, *Study for a Portrait of Empress Josephine*, c. 1804. Executed in shaded black and white chalk on blue paper, Prud'hon's deft study captured to perfection the beauty of the Creole aristocrat Bonaparte married in March 1796. Thanks to this work, the artist received several official commissions. He would become drawing instructor to both Marie-Louise of Austria (Josephine's successor) and the King of Rome, the son of Napoleon and Marie-Louise. Prud'hon also realized the last portrait made of the Emperor during the Hundred Days, thus

completing a series of works dedicated to Napoleonic glory that had begun with an allegory entitled *The Triumph of the First Consul Bonaparte or the Peace*, first shown at the Salon of 1801. In addition to the well-known busts by Chinard (1805) and Bosio (1809), and the various miniatures, there exist numerous portraits of Josephine, among them works by Henri-Robert Riesener (1806), Lethière (1807), and Robert Lefèvre (1808). The most famous portraits, however, are those by François Gérard (*Josephine at Malmaison* [1800] and *Josephine in Coronation Robes* [1806]) and Prud'hon (*Empress Josephine in the Park at Malmaison* [1805–1810] and an unfinished portrait), and Gros (*Josephine at Malmaison* [1809]), who found the subject somewhat fuller in form.

overleaf, pages 52–53: Malmaison, today a museum and pilgrimage site, bears rare witness to the decorative tastes of the Consular period. Thanks to recent work, the ground floor has regained the authentic character it displayed during the residence of Josephine and Bonaparte. The vestibule, seen here, was designed by Percier and Fontaine, the leading architects of the Napoleonic era. Upstairs, on the *étage noble*, only Josephine's apartment retains its décor. The park, now reduced to 15 acres of land, provides little sense of the marvels strewn about the 170 acres it attained during the Empire.

Active period. The Consulate transformed post-Revolutionary France.

left: The Republic was stabilized, with its Germinal franc, which itself would remain stable until World War I. Created by the Convention of 1795, the franc was to be minted according to the law of 17 Germinal XI (17 April 1803). The 1-franc piece had to weigh 5 grams and contain 90 percent silver. Also created were silver pieces worth 5, 2, 0.50, and 0.25 francs as well as gold pieces worth 20 francs (the Napoleon) and even 50 francs. Until 1806, the coins would bear the inscription 'République française' and, beginning in 1804, 'Napoléon empereur.'

above: François Gérard, *The Signing of the Concordat, 15 July 1801.* The Consulate also negotiated the Concordat with the Vatican, which erased the Revolutionary past and re-established Catholicism as the state religion, while also allowing freedom of worship. Gérard was one of the greatest of the official painters regularly commissioned to represent historic occasions. In the study seen here it is interesting to note the already imperial stance adopted by the Consul in contrast to the rather humble attitude of Cardinal Consalvi, the Vatican's envoy.

above: Jean-Baptiste Isabey, *The Visit of the Consul to the Sevenné Cotton Factory in Rouen*, 1802, private collection. With a close eye on economic activity, especially industry and commerce, Bonaparte traveled to Normandy in the autumn of 1802 and visited the Rouen cotton factory operated by the brothers Sevenné. It was his first venture into the provinces since he became Consul for Life. Isabey counted among the artists most involved with the Napoleonic period and the iconography of the great man. In constant demand for official commissions, he produced numerous political and ceremonial portraits.

left: Jean-Antoine Houdon, *Napoleon as Hermes*, 1806. Already famous under the *ancien régime*, Houdon continued to enjoy success, whatever government happened to be in power. He was one of the first artists recruited to make a portrait bust of the First Consul. In 1806 the Imperial couple agreed to pose for him, an encounter that produced the bust at left, with its antique band tied at the back of the head and trailing over the left shoulder. Although meant for translation into marble, the bust would remain in terracotta. Even before Houdon, the idol had been carved in marble and cast in bronze. The best-known of the works are those by Boizot (1800), Chinard (1801), and Corbet (1802). The most celebrated of all may be the heroic nude statue realized by Antonio Canova, completed in 1806 from a study made in 1802. The finished work arrived in Paris in 1811.

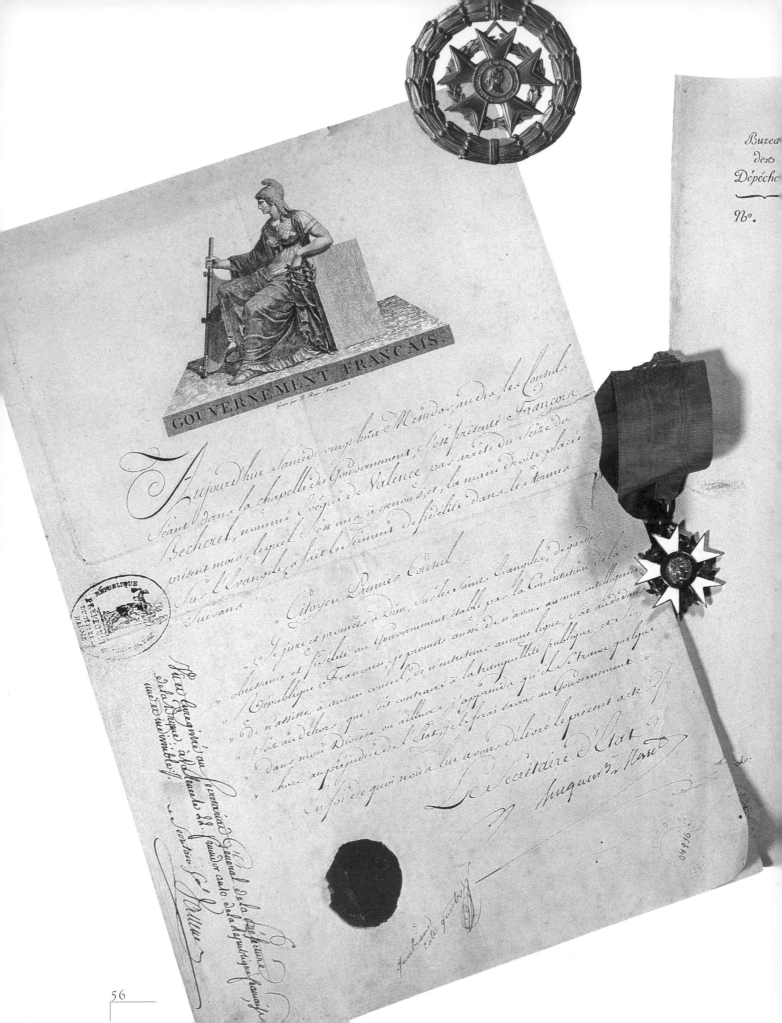

Légion d'honneur.

———◆———

Paris, le 17 Messidor, an 12.

*Le Grand-Chancelier de la
Légion d'honneur,*

X Monsieur L'Évêque de Valence, Membre de
la Légion d'honneur.

L'Empereur, en Grand-Conseil, vient de vous
nommer Membre de la Légion d'honneur.

Je m'empresse et je me félicite vivement,
Monsieur, de vous annoncer ce témoignage de la bienveillance
de Sa Majesté Impériale et de la reconnaissance
nationale.

P.S. Je vous invite à prêter, devant le Président
la Cour ou du Tribunal les plus voisins, le Serment prescrit
par la Loi, ou à m'envoyer, signé de vous, celui dont je joins
la formule.

After abolishing all distinctions in 1791, the Revolution re-established them for the military in the form of honorary sabers. Bonaparte, once in power, instituted a national order for the purpose of recognizing both civil merit and military bravery. The result was a new chivalry composed of elites. Despite rather strong opposition, a decree of 19 May 1802 brought into being the Legion of Honor. In 1808 the order would be integrated with the nobility of the Empire. Between 1802 and 1815, some 35,000 people were decorated. The grades go from Legionaire (*chevalier*) to *grand cordon* or wide sash (dignitaries of the regime). A hierarchy ranks officers, commanders, and major officers. The head of state presides over the order, assisted by a board of directors, and the whole is organized in fifteen territorial sections. The famous star with five double points, the subject of a decree issued on 22 Messidor XII (1 July 1804) and very likely designed by David, is of mysterious origin. Not known is whether the emblem derived from the sign adopted by the Society of Philadelphians, a Masonic lodge with military membership (which, according to Tulard, owes much to the imagination of Nodier in his anonymous work of 1815 entitled *Les Philadelphes: Histoires des sociétés secrètes dans l'armée*), or whether it evokes the star in the ancient arms of the Bonapartes, or yet the star that guided Bonaparte from the Pyramids to the Tuileries. It may also be nothing more than an echo of the royal order of Saint Louis.

below: This engraving represents the oath taken by the members of the Legion of Honor on 15 July 1804.

right: François Gérard, *Bonaparte as First Consul*, February 1803. This portrait reflects a change in the subject's physiognomy, notable in the slightly fuller face and figure, a new softness of expression, as if a smile were about to break. Still, the posture remains erect. The hair, albeit cut short *à la* Titus, falls luxuriantly over the brow. The transition of the image into that of Napoleon seems clearly to be underway.

opposite: Pierre-Joseph Bazin, *Founding of the Education Houses of the Legion of Honor, 20 March 1809*. This late painting, with a largely allegorical theme, reflects the same changes in appearance noted by Gros in his portrait of 1803.

above: Jean-Baptiste Debret, *The First Distribution of the Legion of Honor in the Invalides Church by the Emperor, 15 July 1804*, 1812. Napoleon was now solidly enthroned as he pinned the Croix de Guerre on an aged veteran. The First Consul had become Emperor by *senatus consultum* on 18 May 1804 and by plebiscite in July. The date of 15 July did not in any way compromise the symbolic value of the event. Actually, the 14th fell on a Saturday, and a holiday (Sunday) was needed in order to make a bigger splash. The date confirmed the link between the Revolution, the new regime, already on its way to becoming Imperial, and the distinction of the modern elites.

A CHARLEMAGNE
for modern times

'Napoleon, by the grace of God and the Constitutions of the Republic, Emperor of the French.' The Revolution had now been crowned—to the dismay of many, including Beethoven, who promptly renamed his Third Symphony, calling it the *Eroica* instead of the *Bonaparte*, as originally planned. Nevertheless, a man of the Enlightenment transformed into the great man—the providential person—now embodied, in his own singular way, the first profane universal myth. Charismatic leader, master of war and peace, restorer of Catholicism as state religion, a messiah taking unto himself the symbols of both the Republic and the Roman emperors—all of it would be synthesized in the coronation held on 2 December 1804. Simultanesouly as he insinuated himself among the kings of the *ancien régime*, by having his power sacrelized, Napoleon also swore to maintain the laws born of the Revolution. Without precedent or imitation, the ceremony unfolded in Paris's Notre-Dame Cathedral, fitted out as a Greek temple by the architects Percier and Fontaine. All present—six thousand guests, including every possible dignitary and the entire diplomatic corps—looked in awe upon the 23 meters of Josephine's purple-velvet train, 'held' (not 'carried') by the great man's furious sisters, and the rich coronation robes studded with golden bees and the letter 'N' embroidered about with olive, laurel, and oak leaves. Ceremonial sword at his side and gold laurel crown on his head, Napoleon bore Charlemagne's scepter and the Bourbons' Hand of Justice. On the altar rested the gold crown, the scepter, and the Imperial orb. Back on 7 September 1804 the new Emperor had gone to Aix-la-Chapelle (Aachen) and meditated at the tomb of Charlemagne. All the symbolism marshaled in Notre-Dame referred back to the medieval Emperor of the West.

By crowning himself and then crowning Josephine (the couple religiously wed only the night before), Napoleon avoided appearing as if he had received the Empire from a higher, religious power. Pius VII was left merely to provide benediction and an embrace. Paisiello's *Te Deum*, motets by Lesueur, a *Vivat* from Abbé Roze—the sacred music went hand in hand with a civil ceremony, in which Napoleon took an oath, albeit one the Pope, having already slipped away, did not administer. The Emperor swore to uphold the territorial integrity of the Republic, to impose respect for equal rights, civil liberty, and freedom of religion, for the right of property and the sale of national properties, and to maintain the institution of the Legion of Honor (the first distribution of eagles had taken place on 15 July in the Invalides church).

The Eagle crowned Henceforth two animals would symbolize the Empire: the eagle and the bee. Napoleon's choice of emblems was fixed by a decree signed on 21 Messidor XII (10 July 1804). The eagle was to be preferred over the cock, which the Council of State had favored, as well as over the lion devouring the English leopard proposed by Ségur, the elephant, the oak advocated by Duroc, or even the fleur de lys, which Lebrun insisted stood for France, not the Bourbons, because, as Rome reminded him, it evoked Charlemagne. Seals, acts, and official documents, buildings, robes worn by dignitaries, poles for regimental flags (displaying Jupiter with spindle but no bolt of lightning)—all now bore the Imperial eagle. In 1810 David would immortalize the distribution of eagles to the army on the Champs-de-Mars (5 December 1804), in the presence of the fourteen active Marshals of France (as well as four honorary ones: Kellermann, Lefebvre, Pérignon, and Sérurier), all promoted to that status on 19 May 1804 (Berthier, Murat, Moncey, Jourdan, Masséna, Augereau, Bernadotte, Soult, Brune, Lannes, Mortier, Ney, Davout, Bessières, appointed in that order). As

for the bee, so liked by Cambacérès, it appealed by virtue of its industry but even more for the link it provided between the new dynasty and the origins of France. In 1653 golden bees (actually cicadas!) had been discovered in the tomb of Childéric, the father of Clovis. The Napoleonites therefore identified themselves not only with the Carolingian line but also with the even more ancient Merovingians.

above: Jean-Baptiste Isabey, *Coronation Album* (realized in collaboration with Percier and Fontaine), 1807, private collection. For the coronation there was a veritable mobilization of artists. David himself would paint the climactic scene (pages 64–65).

opposite above: Jacques-Louis David, *Study for a Full-Length Portrait of the Emperor*. David made this nude study in preparation for a portrait that would have been presented to Genoa. After Napoleon rejected the project, it survived as no more than a sketch. The artist may have taken his inspiration from one moment in the coronation, when the Emperor seized the scepter and the Hand of Justice and prepared to descend from the throne.

opposite below: David also designed this two-edged sword for the lead herald (private collection), who used it to proclaim Napoleon Emperor of the French. It was produced at Versailles by Boutet.

On 16 December 1804 a Parisian festival celebrated, in a kind of apotheosis, the accession of Napoleon to the throne. Fireworks re-created the image of Mont St. Bernard—spouting flames like a volcano! The 'Marseillaise,' now out of fashion, gave way to 'Veillons au salut de l'Europe,' in which the last word, signifying state or nation, would henceforth change the meaning:

> *En garde for the safety of the Empire,*
> *En garde for the security of our rights,*
> *Should despotism and tyranny conspire*
> *En garde for the end of kings and knights!*
> *Liberty! Liberty! To thee let every mortel bend a knee,*
> *Tremble, tremble, despots all, account for your disgrace!*
> *Rather death than slavery, the motto we the French embrace!*

A new Charlemagne indeed, but a Charlemagne King of the people. In the *Mémorial*, Las Cases reports this revealing anecdote: 'He says that in returning from his coronation in Italy—somewhere around Lyons—the population ran into the roads. He fantasized that he might, all alone and on foot, climb the Tarare mountain, but permit no one to follow him. Mingling with the crowd, he approached a mature lady and asked her what all this meant. She responded that it was the Emperor who was going to pass that way. Upon which, after a few polite words, he said to her: "But my dear you formerly had the Capet tyrant, now you have the Napoleon tyrant. What in the devil have you gained by all that?" The force of the argument, said Napoleon, disconcerted the lady for a moment. She recovered, however, and replied: "But, excuse me, sir, after all, there is a big difference. We have chosen this one, and we had the other one by accident."'

The cult Following the coronation, a number of elements coalesced around the Emperor and resolved into a cult. There were, of course, the sycophantic writers, who, like Lebrun/Pindar with his odes, sang the praises of the new master. Alongside them came the Church, which in 1806 published the *Imperial Catechism*, all the while the clergy transformed themselves into knowing propagandists for the regime. The 15th of August—the Emperor's birthday, which coincided with the saint's day for an early Christian named Napoleon, martyred under

Diocletian—became a national holiday, observed in
tandem with the traditional feast of the Virgin
Mary. In 1896 the Bishop of Montpellier would go
so far as to declare that 'every time the 15th of
August came round, during the first Empire as well
as during the second . . . even those who were not
believers became accustomed to celebrating the feast
of the Assumption! They liked hearing the blessed
name of the Virgin and blending it into their
thoughts about the old and new glories of their
country.' School instruction, the sanctification of
the army, military parades, the erection of
monuments—everything would serve to promote the
Emperor, god of war. As for monuments, one has
only to think of the Arc de Triomphe du Carrousel,
the Arc de Triomphe de l'Étoile (projected if not
completed), and the statue of Charlemagne intended
for the top of the Vendôme Column but then
replaced by an image of Napoleon in the guise of a
Roman emperor.

opposite: Jacques Bertaux, *Coronation Procession,* c. 1805.
The artist was active precisely during the period of Napoleon's rise
to power. The coach is preserved at Versailles.

opposite and overleaf, pages 64–65: Jacques-Louis David, *The
Coronation of Napoleon I and the Crowning of the Empress
Josephine in Notre-Dame Cathedral in Paris, 2 December 1804,* 1807.
Historically somewhat inaccurate, the immense tableau painted
by David, who was present in Notre-Dame (his self-portrait appears
immediately above Madame Mère, who was in fact absent), is a
pious work of Napoleonic idolatry. Napoleon plays the central role,
at the crossing of the cathedral's main axes, and does so from a
dominant position, both in height and half-way between the Pope
and the Empress. After noting the positions of various participants
on a plan of the cathedral, David painted the Pope, signed the
painting *Napoleonis, Francorum Imperatoris, primarius pictor* (which
would be removed under the Restoration), and spent the year 1805
making sketches and preliminary studies. The picture, also known
as *Le Sacre,* would be finished only in November 1807. On
4 January 1808 Napoleon visited the artist's studio and expressed
his delight: 'This is not a painting; one could walk right into this
picture.' He then lifted one hand to his hat and said 'David, I salute
you,' an extraordinary tribute. The canvas was carried into the great
hall to await exhibition in 1808, when it would be seen alongside
the artist's *Rape of the Sabine Women.*

below: Laurel leaves became a favorite motif, as on this Bank of France medallion engraved by Jean-Pierre Droz in 1809.

left: François Gérard, *Napoleon I in Coronation Robes*, c. 1806. The Emperor presented this portrait, with its gilt frame designed by Ménard, to his sister Caroline Murat.

opposite: Denis-Antoine Chaudet, *Napoleon Legislator*, 1806, Château de Compiègne and Hermitage, St. Petersburg. In this sculpture, commissioned by the Corps Législatif (inaugurated on 14 January 1805), Chaudet remained faithful to his Neoclassical style. He also modeled a bust that would be reproduced in various media—plaster, marble, bronze, biscuit—and the colossal bronze figure placed in 1810 atop the Vendôme Column (initially called the Austerlitz Column and then the Victories Column), it too a Romanized image of the Emperor.

overleaf, pages 66–67: After the coronation, Napoleon's image spread in a truly imperialist manner. Several painters assumed the task of magnifying the Emperor clad in coronation robes. Ingres, in his *Napoleon I on the Imperial Throne* (page 67), evoked a kind of antique majesty, especially in the highly stylized, hieratic pose. Key features are the Carolingian insignia, the scepter of Charles V ('of Charlemagne,' so it was said), the Hand of Justice, the sword created for Napoleon, the 'Merovingian' bees, and the eagle patterned into the rug. Critics, noting the purity of line, the documentary realism of the décor, and the symmetry, reproached Ingres for his 'gothicism.' On the facing page (66) appears an Imperial portrait by Anne-Louis Girodet, who also represented the Emperor in coronation attire, his right hand raised above the Imperial emblems and the Napoleonic Code and his left hand grasping the scepter surmounted by an eagle. Girodet was then commissioned to paint thirty-six copies of the portrait, for placement in Imperial residences and for use as gifts. By 1814 twenty-six of the copies had been completed; they remained with the artist until after his death.

opposite: Andrea Appiani, *Napoleon, King of Italy*, 1805. Still more laurel leaves, this time in a portrait of Napoleon attired for his coronation in Milan as King of Italy (26 May 1805). After 1796, when he first encountered the young conqueror of Italy, Appiani came in for considerable fame and fortune. Here the Emperor and King of Italy is more simply got up than he had been for the Paris *sacre*. The ensemble comprises a green-velvet coat embroidered in gold, a green cape studded with small silver flowers and lined with white satin, the collar and lapels embroidered in gold, and white gloves, these too gold-embroidered. The sword slipped under the sash about the waist terminates in a head of Mercury and an eagle. The expression on the subject's face repeats that found in Appiani's earlier portraits of Bonaparte.

above, left and right: Jean-Baptiste Isabey, *Napoleon, Emperor and King of Italy*, c. 1805. The preparatory study and painting alike show Napoleon dressed in his *petit costume de cour*. Smaller or simpler though it may be, this court dress is a far cry from the simplicity captured by Isabey in his portrait of Bonaparte at Malmaison (page 49) as well as from the clothing worn by Bonaparte in his role as First Consul (page 46).

left: In this bronze portrait-bust Napoleon wears the Iron Crown of the Lombard kings, the very one, in fact, worn by Charlemagne and that Napoleon had placed upon his own head in Milan Cathedral. The Iron Crown is so called because of the nail from the True Cross melted and cast into the interior band. Napoleon reportedly declared: 'God grants it to me; woe to him who touches it.'

The emblems symbolizing the Empire 'for eternity' appear on all manner of supports.

left: Grand Imperial arms from the throne used by Napoleon during his visit to Strasbourg in 1805 (private collection).

below: Grand Imperial arms of the Emperor designed by David for the coronation (carved wood; private collection).

opposite, above and right: The Imperial bee on a lampas produced in 1812 by Grand Frères for the Emperor's large salon at Versailles (private collection) and on a foot cushion made for the coronation by Picot, embroiderer by appointment to the Emperor. Picot also, and most notably, executed the attire worn by Napoleon at the Paris coronation (private collection).

opposite, below: Project for a sabretache designed by Carle Vernet for Eugène de Beauharnais at the Paris coronation (private collection). After the proclamation of the Empire, Vernet became responsible for flags and standards, which, once approved by Napoleon, would be signed and then consigned to Picot.

At the heart of Napoleon's Imperial symbolism were the eagle and the bee. At the coronation, the purple robes worn by Napoleon and Josephine as well as the tapestries hung in Notre-Dame were scattered over with golden bees. 'A republic with a leader' was how Cambacérès and Lacuée characterized bee society when they went before the Council of State to justify the bee as a symbol of the reign. Their source: the Merovingian monarchs. As for the eagle, the heraldists of the 17th century had already noted the association of the eagle with Charlemagne dating back to the 13th century. Vivant Denon and Napoleon read all the relevant texts before creating the Empire's armorial bearings (the subject of a decree issued on 10 July 1804). The Napoleonic eagle, its wings lowered, clutches a bolt of lightning. The eagles on flags would be natural birds, their wings slightly spread, the left claw holding a Jupiter spindle without lightning. The reference to Roman antiquity was clearly intended.

above: Jacques-Louis David, *The Oath Sworn by the Army to the Emperor after the Distribution of Eagles on the Champ-de-Mars, 5 December 1804*, 1810. Begun in 1808, David's great painting could be seen as a pendant to the *Sacre*, completed in 1807 (pages 64–65). Behind the Emperor, arrayed in his coronation robes, is a seated cluster of dignitaries, sisters, sisters-in-law, and ambassadors. Josephine, though initially included, is absent, Napoleon having by now married Marie-Louise of Austria. In the foreground stand the Marshals, Lannes looking at Napoleon. On the right, delegates from the regiments tip their newly received flags, accompanied by generals and officers. In a preparatory study, David had envisioned a winged victory scattering laurel leaves over the assembled company. Napoleon insisted that it be removed.

opposite: Gioacchino Giuseppe Serangeli, *The Emperor Receiving Deputations from the Army in the Antiquities Hall at the Musée Napoléon in the Louvre on 9 December 1804*, 1808. Commissioned in May 1807, this painting would be ready for the Salon of the following year. Murat and Bessière stand at right, while on the left appear Louis Bonaparte, Berthier, Joseph Bonaparte, Cambarcérès, and Lebrun.

right: In 1806 a Saint Napoleon, supposedly a victim of Diocletian's persecution of early Christians, was exhumed. His feast day, already fixed on 15 August, became a national holiday in France. Since the Concordat was also celebrated on this date, the amalgam could not have been more complete. In truth, however, it was the cult of Napoleon himself—restorer of religion, savior of the Church, anointed sovereign, living saint—who was celebrated.

SALLE DES SAISONS.

IMPERATOR
master of Europe

The *Bulletins de la Grande Armée*, one of the instruments of propaganda most immediately conducive to the legend, existed to report the Imperial epic step by step and thus give effective voice to the god of war, a god with an eye ever fixed on posterity. The first issue appeared on 7 October 1805 and the last on 20 June 1815, the day after the Battle of Waterloo. In theory a weekly publication, the *Bulletins* appeared at various intervals, depending upon military events. Printed, sometimes with illustrations, the issues would also be reproduced in newspapers and read in villages and theatres, even in church sermons and high-school lectures. The future Romantic generation was rocked to sleep with lullabies entoned in a male, Napoleonic accent. Louis-Léopold Boilly's *Reading the Seventh Bulletin*, a picture somewhat after the manner of Greuze, depicts a French family checking a map while reading the account of a battle. The 29th *Bulletin*, notable for its coverage of the Berezina crossing (a dreadful episode during the retreat from Moscow), ends with 'the health of His Majesty has never been better'; nonetheless, it captures for all time the legendary image of the holy squadron camped about the person of Napoleon.

Mars's own protégé knew instinctively how to make himself loved by his men. We have only to recall that famous night before Austerlitz, on 1 December 1805, when the soldiers lit straw torches and promised to celebrate the anniversary of their commander's coronation by bringing back every last enemy flag. By 1807 a certain amount of grumbling could be heard; never mind, the Grand Army always marched as ordered. Even in 1813 Napoleon found himself enthusiastically received. The Waterloo forces loved their Emperor, around whom the very troops sent against him rallied all the way from Golfe-Juan to Paris in March 1815. Anecdotes of this sort, many of them more or less concocted, would fuel the legend throughout the 19th century.

above: Pierre Gautherot, *Napoleon Addressing the Second Corps of the Grand Army on the Lech Bridge at Augsburg, 12 October 1805.* Veneration by the troops, charismatic commander at stage center, his gesture calm and assured—such are the formal and ideological themes taken up in this painting, and effectively so.

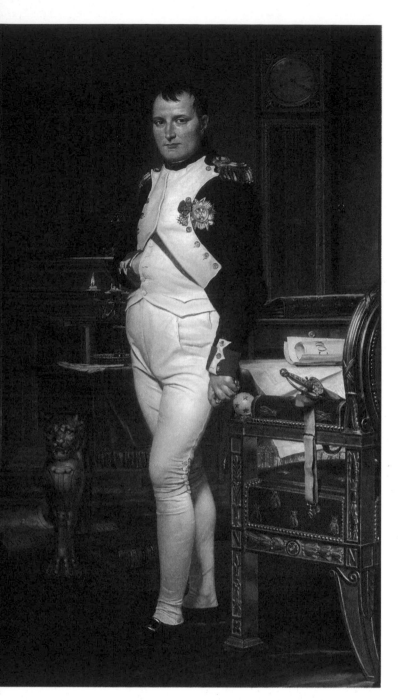

above: Jacques-Louis David, *Napoleon in His
Study at the Tuileries*, 1812. This time David
portrayed the Emperor as legislator, hard at work
in his study. The commission had come from
England's Duke of Hamilton, a great admirer of
Napoleon. According to David's image, the
Emperor has spent the night composing his
Code Napoléon, totally unaware that dawn has
come, evident in the low-burning or guttered
candles and the clock, which has just struck
four in the morning. He rises to buckle on his
sword and go review the troops.

The immortal brigades found a permanent home in
the heroic imagination of the French.

The arts in service to the master By 1806 the
Imperial court was well established, its successful
image of power based upon models found not only
in France but also abroad. Moreover, it satisfied the
desire of Napoleon that his sovereignty be identified
with an active judiciary, as well as with the pomp and
ceremony of a new nobility, to be created in 1808.
Crucial to that image were the contributions of a
group of gifted artists prepared to represent the
great man in a vast range of powerful portraits and
epic scenes. While David and Gros endowed the hero
with an air of calm control, other painters offered
images steeped in allegory (a Napoleonic genre
already developed by Prud'hon in 1801) or pictures
idealizing the Emperor. Among the allegorists, Callet
distinguished himself in his vision of the Austerlitz
victory and in his view of Napoleon as an armor-clad
Apollonian figure driving a chariot. In battle scenes
the tendency was to privilege the commander,
whereas older canvases, dating from the first to the
second Italian campaigns, focused mainly on the
army— France in arms—with the General caught up
in the overall melee. Beginning with Marengo (14
June 1800), the hero would occupy stage center,
most notably in a work painted by Carle Vernet in
1804. Louis-François Lejeune, a military artist,
organized his *Napoleon Bivouacked on the Eve of Austerlitz*
around an Emperor whose erect silhouette against a
background of billowing white smoke becomes the
focal point. Sometimes warrior, sometimes
magistrate, the Consul with hair styled in the
manner of Emperor Titus evolved more and more
into the great man deep into his thoughts and
idealized in feature. The Salons played a major role,
and Napoleon never missed one. Here he saw himself
portrayed as the seigneur of war, with or without his
greatcoat, a charismatic, marmoreal figure showing
magnanimity towards an adversary converted into an
ally (Debret, *Napoleon I at Tilsit Decorating a Soldier of the
Russian Army with the Cross of the Legion of Honor, 9 July*

1807 [1808]) or compassion either for his victims or for a wounded friend (Bourgeois, *The Last Moments of General Lannes at the Battle of Essling, 22 May 1809*). In this regard, Gros's *Napoleon Visiting the Battlefield at Eylau, 9 February 1807* is exemplary, a scene of frozen horror. On the other hand, Meynier's *The Return of Napoleon to the Isle of Lobau Following the Battle of Essling on 23 May 1809* (1812) presents a Napoleon rather coldly blessing the wounded, a scene remote from the *Pesthouse at Jaffa*. On the other hand, the commander was sometimes depicted among his men, as in Roehn's *Bivouac on the Battlefield at Wagram on the Night of 5–6 July 1809* (1810), where Napoleon is treated as a figure already legendary, a hero dozing in a chair, twilit and watched by his faithful Marshals, the latter attentive, full of admiration and love. The Emperor was painted in majesty, as the Prince of Peace, a sacred idol (Ingres, *Napoleon I on the Imperial Throne* [1806]), or yet in epic or hieratic poses. Gérard's *Napoleon I in Coronation Robes* (1805) would be copied again and again, for reproduction on the money issued by the Interior Ministry or for placement in French embassies abroad. In 1812 Girodet received a commission to paint thirty-six copies of his full-length *Portrait of the Emperor in Coronation Robes*, several

of which were given in 1809 to dignitaries or to members of the Imperial family. Then too there was the role of Napoleon as King of Italy, first captured in an 1805 portrait by Appiani, who represented the subject wearing the *petit* ceremonial attire made for the coronation in Milan. The apogee of the Empire, as well as perhaps the beginning of the end, can be seen in David's *Napoleon in His Study at the Tuileries* (1812), a realistic image of the Emperor as a workaholic. The times and the burdens had left their mark. Napoleon, dressed in the blue uniform of a colonel of the grenadier guard, presents a rather puffy face, the hair thin, the figure grown plump; yet he remains imposing by virtue of his authority and the apparent omnipotence of a Promethean hero.

Brilliant star All of the above fell within the realm of official iconography, clearly constituent parts of the legend, with elements of the myth elevated through aspects of universal symbolism. Napoleon also saw himself carved in marble and cast in bronze, reluctant as he was to be turned into a statue. The antique carried the day, best seen in a bust by Antoine-Denis Chaudet. Already the First Consul had commissioned a series of busts as embellishments for the Tuileries, bringing together the great men of antiquity, the *ancien régime*, and the Revolution. The Emperor had the Salle des Maréchaux decorated, and for the Louvre he featured the princes and dignitaries of his own regime. The overall purpose was to glorify a modern reign and a modern genius.

Opera brought the hero to the lyric stage as a conquering, legislative, civilizing force. It was literature, however, that most effectively expressed the values of the Empire. Napoleon, of course, understood that he had 'minor literature' on his side and 'great literature' against him. Poetry offered grandiloquent odes. Theatre favored tragedy, performed triumphantly by Talma, the Empire's favorite actor and a sincere friend to Napoleon. Today it is easy enough to mock the fawning poets and the obsequious dramatists. We should note, however, that while the great writers of the period— among them Chateaubriand and Mme de Staël—did indeed identify with the opposition, it was Napoleon who ushered in the French era in the modern world, thus prolonging and spreading the brilliance of the Enlightenment brought to the world by 18th-century France. The Emperor imposed his image on the universe, an image subject to numerous metamorphoses but also bound to eternity.

opposite above: Giuseppe Borsato, *Entrance of Napoleon into Venice, 29 November 1807.* Here the artist proved himself to be a latter-day Canaletto.

opposite below: Charles-Auguste-Guillaume Steuben, *Napoleon I Wearing the Insignia of the Iron Crown and the Legion of Honor*, 1812. By the time of this portrait Napoleon has gained weight. The combination of the two decorations symbolized the union of the Empire and the Kingdom of Italy. The Order of the Iron Crown. instituted after the Milanese coronation in 1805, was considered the equivalent of France's Legion of Honor, complete with three degrees: chevalier, commander, and dignitary.

above: Charles Meynier, *Entrance of Napoleon into Berlin, 27 October 1806*, Salon 1810. The Empire imposed its laws, including its revolutionary liberties, all over the Continent, as Napoleon entered one capital after another. The scene depicted here occurred in numerous cities with high symbolic import. Meynier's painting was one of several that commemorated the seizures and ritual affirmations of power.

overleaf, page 82: Antoine-Jean Gros, *Napoleon Visiting the Battlefield at Eylau, 9 February 1807*, 1808. With this huge canvas, Gros, a Baron of the Empire, more or less sounded the opening chord of Romanticism, by doing justice to the tragic slaughter at Eylau. The scene is one of frozen desolation and quasi-holy horror, both poignant and gripping, redeemed by the compassion and clemency of an Emperor appalled at the vastness of what is a veritable cemetery.

Napoleon: *The Immortal Emperor*

overleaf, page 83: Pierre Gautherot, *Napoleon Wounded before Ratisbonn, 23 April 1809*, Salon 1810. After the Emperor suffered a wound in Germany, Gautherot was commissioned to record the event for display at the Tuileries. Napoleon, calm as usual, behaves like a modern Achilles, manifesting quiet heroism and impatient to remount his horse.

overleaf, pages 84–85: Of all the victories won by Napoleon, Austerlitz is without doubt the one that remains most central to his legend. Abundantly illustrated in painting, as well as in thousands of engravings, prints, drawings, and the popular *images d'Épinal*, the battle could very well be reconstructed chronologically from a whole series of pictures.

page 84, above: Louis-François Lejeune, *Napoleon Bivouacked on the Eve of Austerlitz, 1 December 1805*. Lejeune, with genuine realism, re-created the ambiance of a military camp, including the barouche in which Napoleon spent the night and an orderly saddling the master's white horse. At center the Emperor receives villagers, who could be informants or plaintiffs.

page 84, below: Carle Vernet, *Napoleon Giving Orders the Morning of the Battle of Austerlitz*.

page 85, above: François Gérard, *The Battle of Austerlitz, 2 December 1805*, Salon 1810. This painting, Gérard's sole venture into the battle genre, was extremely well received, even officially by Napoleon. To officers who missed the battle, he would have advised: 'Go see, messieurs, how we were at Austerlitz.'

page 85, below: Carle Vernet, *The Battle of Austerlitz, 2 December 1805*. Here the conquered surrender their flags to the conqueror.

above: Anne-Louis Girodet, *Napoleon Receives the Keys to the City of Vienna, 14 November 1805*. The depicted event actually took place before the stunning victory at Austerlitz.

left: Jean-Baptiste Isabey and others, *The Austerlitz Table*, 1806–1811. Unofficially and incorrectly, the work seen here is called the 'Table of Marshals,' because of the circle of medallion portraits, all busts, disposed about a portrait of the Emperor in coronation robes. However, only eleven of the medallions represent marshals, a rank never attained by Duroc and Coulaincourt, who complete the total of thirteen. All are identified by their nobiliary titles given in labels below the images.

overleaf, pages 88–89: Casanova *fils* (Alexandre Dufay),
*The Marriage Banquet of Napoleon and Marie-Louise in the Hall
of Spectacles at the Tuileries Palace, 2 April 1810*, c. 1811. Having
become Emperor, Napoleon was eager to found a dynasty by divorcing
the childless Josephine and marrying Archduchess Marie-Louise,
daughter of Francis I of Austria. The event generated a number of
official representations, including the one seen here.

opposite: Marie-Guillemine Benoît, *Marie-Louise, Empress of France.*
c. 1811. Napoleon's second wife, despite the many portraits and
objects made to promote her image, never acquired the prestige
enjoyed by Josephine.

left: Bosio (Manufacture Impériale de Sèvres), *Portrait Bust of Marie-
Louise*, private collection.

below: Picot, embroiderer to the Emperor, created this *corbeille
d'atours* (finery basket) as a wedding present for Marie-Louise in 1810
(private collection).

bottom: Nito fashioned this watch for the new Empress around 1810.

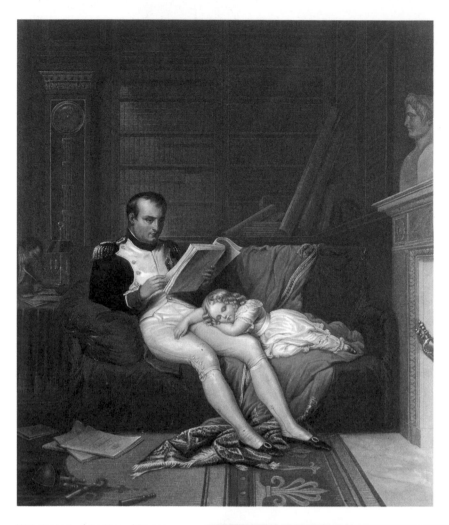

In addition to the famous portrait of the King of Rome by Prud'hon, who visualized the child as a sleeping Cupid, a number of representations came from the official painters.

below: Jean-Baptiste Isabey, *The Infant King of Rome*, c. 1813, private collection. Working in the manner of a miniaturist, Isabey made this portrait for Marie-Louise, who then presented it to Mme de Montesquiou, the child's governess.

bottom: Innocent Goubaud, *The Infant King of Rome*, private collection. The artist would become the young Prince's drawing instructor.

With the birth of the King of Rome in 1811, the Napoleonic regime seemed to have assured its dynastic continuity. One of history's victims, this Imperial child, so often the subject of portraits, would enter the legend only much later in the century, after he had become l'Aiglon (the Eaglet), thanks to *L'Aiglon* (1900), a celebrated play by Edmond Rostand.

opposite: Georges Rouget, *The Birth of the King of Rome, 20 March 1811*, Salon 1812. Napoleon proudly presents his newborn son to the dignitaries of the Empire.

above: This intimate scene was one of many compositions involving the 'divine child' in a way that would appeal to bourgeois or middle-class sentiment.

ISLAND TO ISLAND
the fall, the return, the martyrdom

1811: Marie-Louise gives birth to the King of Rome; France boasts 130 departments. 1812: the Grand Army faces catastrophe in Russia. 1813: the Napoleonic Empire collapses. 1814: the Allies invade France. Nine years earlier, Austerlitz (1805), the battle of three Emperors, had made Napoleon the master of Europe. In 1813 Leipzig, the battle of nations, saw the whole of Europe turn against him. On the 20th of April 1814 the most poignant scene of the entire epic unfolded in the forecourt of the Château de Fontainebleau:

> Soldiers of my Old Guard, I bid your farewell. For twenty years I have seen you constantly on the road to honor and victory [or 'glory' as some versions would have it]. In more recent times, just as in those of our prosperity, you have not ceased to be models of bravery and fidelity. With men such as you, our cause was never lost. But the war was interminable. There had been the civil war, and it had made France ever more wretched. I therefore sacrificed all our interests to those of the country I now leave. You, my friends, continue to serve France. Her happiness was my sole thought; it shall always be the object of my desires! Do not regret my fate. If I consented to survive, it is to go on serving your glory. I wish to write about the great things we have done together! Adieu my children! I should like to press you all to my heart; at least I can kiss your flag!

After embracing General Petit and kissing the pennant of the Guard, Napoleon departed for a new legend. In 1825 Horace Vernet would paint the moving farewells. Of the Empire, all that remained to the fallen giant was a bit of confetti, the Isle of Elba. But what an Antaeus! From Elba, Napoleon would gather new forces.

On 1 March 1815 Napoleon, having eluded his island captors, landed at Golfe-Juan on the French Riviera. Twenty days later he would be in Paris. A complete and stupendous reversal of situation, one of whose more famous episodes Wilhelm Sternberg immortalized by giving these words to the resurrected commander: 'Soldiers of the fifth regiment, listen to me! If any one of you wishes to kill his General, his Emperor, he can do it. Here I am!' The year 1811 had brought not only the great comet and the birth of the future Aiglon but also a musical production at the Théâtre Feydeau, where Parisians could hear:

> Le mois de mars a, de la France
> À jamais fixé le bonheur.
> C'est la saison de l'Espérance
> Qui donne au trône un successeur.

Best not to forget, however, that this fortunate month had been named for the god of war. Now it seems clear that the 20th of March 1815 already had within it the outlines of what would come on the 18th of June 1815.

The Hundred Days The Hundred Days scarcely allowed artists enough time to record, either on canvas or in stone, their impressions of a period so fraught with concentrated drama. However, popular

left: Anonymous, *Coats Off!*, 1813. This English colored engraving depicts an episode that occurred during the retreat from Russia, an event very likely not emphasized in contemporary French iconography.

below: Serri Gaetano, after François Bouchot, *The Abdication of Napoleon I, 6 April 1814*, c. 1840, Musée Historique de Versailles. Napoleon abdicated twice, first on the 4th of April and then again on the 6th. Initially the Marshals settled the terms, but Napoleon insisted upon preserving the rights of his son, the King of Rome. The Allies, however, wanted an unconditional abdication in exchange for sovereignty over the Isle of Elba. Again urged by the Marshals, Napoleon resigned and signed the following statement: 'The Allied powers, having declared the Emperor Napoleon to be the sole obstacle to the re-establishment of peace in Europe, the Emperor Napoleon, true to his oath, declares that he renounces, for himself and his heirs, the thrones of France and Italy, and that there is no sacrifice, even that of life itself, that he is not prepared to make in the interest of France.' The painting reproduced here—depicting the abdication scene at Fontainebleau—was commissioned by King Louis-Philippe for the historical museum then being assembled at the Château de Versailles.

imagery and engravings proved more adept, seizing the moment and quickly establishing the essentials of contemporary iconography. Escaping one island and ending up on another, soaring like a meteor only to plummet in a flash, traveling from the Rhône valley to the dreary plain, Napoleon replayed his own history, this time at lightning speed.

Although a mere trimester, the Hundred Days became a legend unto themselves. Yes, the Eagle flew from steeple to steeple, all the way to the towers of Notre-Dame, his arrival announced by the proclamation made at Golfe-Juan on 1 March. The Napoleonic genius for memorable phrasing illuminated for all time this blazing surge against the tide of history. Not only did the Emperor attempt to retake the reins of his own destiny, as if 1814 had been nothing more than a temporary setback; he also, even while renouncing all dreams of conquest, identified himself with the humiliated nation, with its people, with the glory of the Revolution—indeed with the last twenty-five years, from the storming of the Bastille in July 1789 to that day in March 1815. He asserted the legitimacy of the Revolution against the *ancien régime*. But let us hear it in his own words:

Soldiers, in my exile I heard your voice. I have overcome all obstacles and every peril. Your General, called to the throne by the choice of the people and carried high on your shoulders, has come to you. Now come and join him.
Seize these colors which the nation has proscribed [the white cockade] and which, for twenty-five years, served as a rallying point for all the enemies of France! Display that tricolore rosette. You carried it in our great times! We must forget that we have been the masters of nations; but we must not allow anyone to meddle in our affairs. Who claims to be our masters? Who would have the power? (*À l'armee.*)

Ascended to the throne by your choice, everything that has been done without you is illegitimate. For twenty-five years France has had new interests, new institutions, a new glory, which cannot be guaranteed except by a national government and by a dynasty born of new circumstances. (*Au peuple français.*)

Napoleon tried to negotiate a new contract with the French and to reassure Europe. They were not having it. The populace received him enthusiastically, but

above, left: Anonymous engraving (Nuremberg), *Napoleon Leaving France for the Isle of Elba*. Like the Battle of Austerlitz, Napoleon's journey from France to Elba and back could be narrated through contemporary images of every move along the way.

opposite above: Joseph Beaum, *Napoleon Departing Portofarraio for a Return to Power*, 1836. On 26 February 1815 Napoleon boarded a ship at Elba's port city for the purpose of regaining power in France.

above, right: Ambroise-Louis Garnery, *Napoleon's Flotilla Sailing Towards the South of France*. On his return journey to France, Napoleon sailed on the brig *Inconstant*, along with a small flotilla of ships carrying 1,100 men. He would disembark at Golfe-Juan on 1 March 1815.

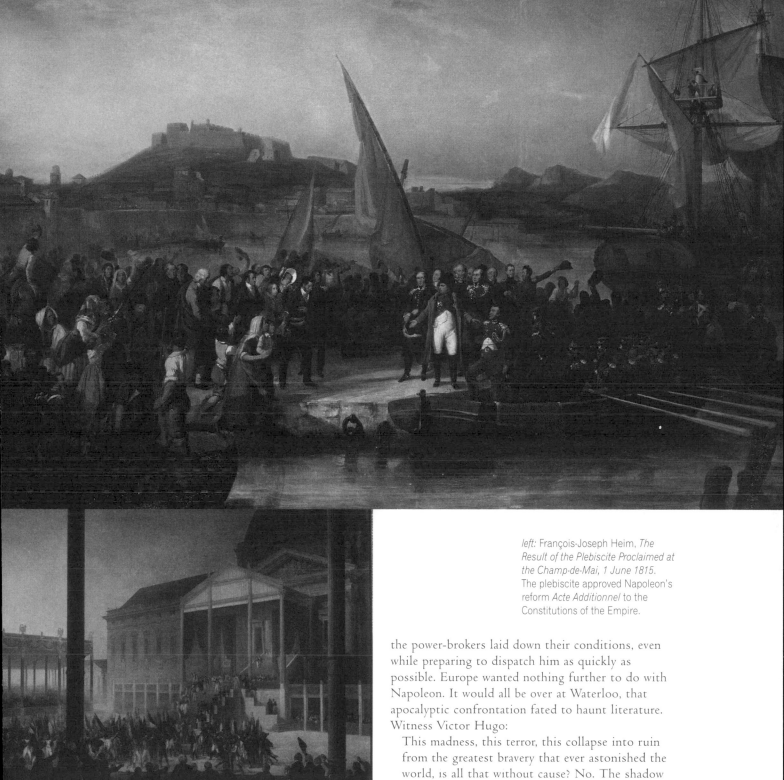

the power-brokers laid down their conditions, even while preparing to dispatch him as quickly as possible. Europe wanted nothing further to do with Napoleon. It would all be over at Waterloo, that apocalyptic confrontation fated to haunt literature. Witness Victor Hugo:

This madness, this terror, this collapse into ruin from the greatest bravery that ever astonished the world, is all that without cause? No. The shadow of an enormous right hand falls upon Waterloo. It is the day of destiny. A force greater than men gave us that day. From it the bowing, horrified heads; from it all the great souls surrendering their swords. Those who had conquered Europe are fallen to the ground, having nothing more to say or do, sensing a terrible presence lurking in the darkness. *Hoc erat in fatis* [Such was destiny]. That

Napoleon's proclamation issued at Golfe-Juan on 1 March 1815. Once again Napoleon showed himself to be a propagandist of genius and a master of rhetoric: 'The Eagle, with the national colors, shall fly from steeple to steeple all the way to the towers of Notre-Dame.'

day, the perspective of humanity changed course. Waterloo, it is the hinge of the 19th century. The disappearance of the great man was necessary to the advent of the great century. One who is unanswerable was in charge. The panic of the hero is understandable. At the Battle of Waterloo, there was more than clouds; there was also a meteor. God passed over. (*Les Misérables*.)

Everything was now ready for the final act of the Napoleonic destiny, bound to the rock of St. Helena, and for the apotheosis of the legend as well as the regeneration of the myth.

The Christ of St. Helena

On 9 August 1815 Napoleon set sail for the tiny island whose existence he had noted in one of his school notebooks. It would be futile to ask what might have been the outcome if Europe had accepted the return from Elba, an hypothesis of scant probability. Meanwhile, the defeated Emperor took pleasure in recalling: 'What a fatality that my return from the Isle of Elba was not sustained! That not everyone saw me as the proper person and the most necessary for the equilibrium and repose of Europe! But the kings and the peoples feared me; they were wrong and could

pay dearly for it. I was becoming a new man; they could not believe it; they could not imagine that a man might have had a soul strong enough to change his character, or bend to necessary circumstances. I had, however, submitted my proofs and given several pledges of this sort. Who does not know that I am not a man given to half-measures? I would have been completely the monarch of the Constitution and the peace, as I had been the monarch of dictatorship and grand enterprises.'

While thus leaving both kings and people to the judgment of history, Napoleon also arrayed himself in the costume of his last role, playing the final apotheosis: 'I have worn the Imperial crown of France, the iron crown of Italy, and now England has given me one even grander and more glorious—that worn by the Savior of the world—a crown of thorns.' Christ and Prometheus, both at the same time, as Las Cases would note in the entry for 15 October 1815 in the *Mémorial de Sainte-Hélène*, a book soon to become the bible of the 19th century: 'Seventy days after leaving England, and one hundred ten after leaving Paris, we dropped anchor around noon. It touches bottom, the first link in the chain that will nail the modern Prometheus to his rock.'

In Plymouth harbor, aboard the ship selected for his last voyage, Napoleon had already begun to dictate his memoirs, with Las Cases there piously collecting every word uttered by a proscribed god. The Emperor, aware that henceforth he must work for posterity, set about to shape his own tomb, summoning the 19th century even in his exile. The writing would take the form of a day-by-day transcription, like thought in the process of evolving as it integrates experience. Moreover, the speaker would stake out a position in and on history. Instead of hagiography, he offered the intimate union of high-flying words, seeming to control the course of events, and the musings of a broken man, a vanquished and humiliated hero. With the Promethean myth he combined the cynicism of a leader stripped of all illusions about men. The individual born of the people took on the demiurge of modernity. From the past Napoleon drew lessons for the future. Reflecting upon his mistakes, very deftly acknowledged, he retraced the path of a most uncommon destiny. The conqueror dialogued with the great men and, playing the victim, explored his pathetic island. It was all part of a construction, a production featuring a Napoleon both profoundly human and sublimely superhuman. The *Mémorial*, a poem about defeated grandeur and an albatross confronted by mediocrities, creates the illusion of having comprehended a warrior in love with peace, a conqueror become the friend of nations, a revolutionary despot. Where propaganda failed, disingenuous literature succeeded. It was the last victory, the ultimate sun of Austerlitz. It would brighten the horizon of a waiting French public.

Towards the assumption of the golden legend

While their Little Corporal paced in circles on his rock, the former members of the Grand Army were launching into a new conquest, that of the heart of the French people. Beginning in 1817 there appeared a series called the *Victoires et Conquêtes des Français*, written by Beauvais, Thiébault, and Parisot, together with the whole of the *Bulletins de la Grande Armée*. Then came the litany of *Mémoires* and *Souvenirs*, from more than a thousand participants in the Consulate and Empire, many of them military men, who wanted to bear witness.

Most of all it was the moment of the Old Guard and the half-paid soldiers, together a living challenge to the Restoration regime, prestigious veterans who spilled into streets and cafés, asking each another if they believed in Jesus Christ and his resurrection, recounted to anyone prepared to listen—and they were numerous—their exploits and the battles of the Empire, exchanged the drawings of Charlet, and distributed images evoking St. Helena or showing the profile of the Other in bouquets of wild pansies. They also hummed the songs of Pierre-Jean de Béranger (for example, 'Le Vieux Drapeau' and 'Les Souvenirs du peuple' [1820]: 'Parlez-nous de lui, grand-mère. Parlez-nous de lui') as well as those of Émile Debraux ('Ah! qu'on est fier d'être Français / Quand on regarde la Colonne!' [1818]), and his 'Te souviens-tu?,' or yet 'Fanfan la Tulipe,' or again 'Partant pour la Syrie,' the troubadour song composed in 1810 by Queen Hortense, a number that would become an official hymn under the Second Empire. The half-pay soldier (*demi-solde*), that 'military bohemian' as the historian Jacques Vidalence put it, a type wonderfully rendered by the painter Géricault, went about with his back straight and his features weathered, dressed in his threadbare greatcoat, gnarled cane in hand and a red ribbon in

top: Anonymous print, *A Dauphinois Grenadier Saluting the Returned Emperor.* The journey that carried the Eagle to the towers of Notre-Dame in early 1815 is strewn with legendary episodes such as the one depicted here.

above: Wilhelm Sternberg, *If Anyone Wishes to Kill His Emperor, Here I Am.* After a battalion from the fifth regiment of infantry attempted the block the road, Napoleon got down from his horse, stepped forward, and announced: 'Soldiers of the fifth line, listen to me! If any one of you wishes to kill his General, his Emperor, he can do it. Here I am!' With shouts of *Vive l'Empereur!*, the battalion fell upon the Little Corporal and embraced him.

his buttonhole. Already during the late years of Napoleon's reign the tendency to exalt the soldier was beginning to set in. The image had now become one of the century's major icons.

Indeed, a war of images had commenced. The forbidden image and the banished symbols found their way into circulation through dissimulation. Snuffboxes, knobs on canes, outlined profiles, likenesses carved into coconuts or bits of wood, greeting signs—all the above were in place and ready for the return from Elba. After Waterloo, it all disappeared and went under cover. Rumblings, rumors, impostors—the myth of a new return always found fresh nourishment. And when the death of the Emperor was officially announced, many there were who refused to believe it. Periodically, knowledge certain held that he had survived, that he was even in France, or in America.

The tomb on the island

5 May 1821: Napoleon breathed his last, setting off the storm winds of the Romantic legend. The Napoleonic cult gained new momentum. Chateaubriand, a fascinated adversary who wrote *Mémoires d'outre-tombe* as an anti-*Mémorial*, found the apt expression: 'Bonaparte was so strongly given to absolute domination that after having suffered the despotism of his person, we must now suffer the despotism of his memory.' Yes, Napoleon would loom extraordinarily large in the collective memory. Already prints were glorifying the dead man on his bed of apotheosis. Already the idealized Napoleon had imposed his image. Horace Vernet was the leading painter of the posthumous glory. From 1821, the first canvas—a prototype work—would be known by two titles: *The Dream of Bertrand* and *The Apotheosis of Napoleon*. Together they reflected the double nature of this modern *chanson de geste*, a dream, if there ever was one, and an allegorical-religious exaltation of the great man. Celebration of a Passion and a Transfiguration, the painting depicts Montholon on his feet sobbing and bent towards the tearful Bertrand family. On the freshly excavated tomb rest Napoleon's sword and hat. On one side, a broken chain symbolizes the deliverance of Prometheus set free by death. In the foreground, the remains of a shipwreck with a plank emblazoned: 'Rivoli, Piramides [sic], Marengo, Austerlitz, Jena [sic], Wagram, Moscova, Montmirail, Ligny, Wat . . .' On the right stand the dead Marshals—Lannes, Berthier, Brune—together with Selim III of Egypt kneeling before the seated Desaix, Poniatowski and Bessières behind them. The shades of the warriors

prepare to receive their commander in the Imperial Valhalla. Clearly the painting had been inspired by Girodet's *Apotheosis of the French Heroes Dead for the Nation during the War of Liberation*. Vernet combined all the symbols of the legend: exile, martyrdom, redemption, fall, glorification, epic, memory, the cult. In 1825 he would portray Napoleon on his deathbed, where the handsome visage—rejuvenated and laurel-wreathed— reflects truth less than the desire to immortalize a Christ-like face.

> *Always him! Him everywhere! Cold or burning,*
> *That ubiquitous image forever in my spirit churning.*
> *My brain it floods with urgent, creative splendor.*
> *I thrill and quake as words on my lips abound*
> *When his aureoled name, glorious in its sound,*
> *Surges up, spilling into my verses its full grandeur.*
> Victor Hugo, 'Him/Lui' (1828)

above: Popular engraving, *Napoleon, on the Île d'Aix, Departs for St. Helena, 15 July 1815*, c. 1833. Ironically, the composition used here is organized along the same lines already employed to depict Louis XVIII as he left Paris for Ghent at the beginning of the Hundred Days. In both scenes a tender-hearted grenadier covers his face.

opposite: Charles Lock Eastlake, *Napoleon on the* Northumberland *Prior to His Departure for St. Helena*, 1815. The HMS *Bellerophon*, with Napoleon on board, arrived in Plymouth harbor on 16 July 1815. The banished Emperor would remain there until the HMS *Northumberland* could be made ready for the voyage to the faraway island prison. Eastlake painted the work seen here on board the *Northumberland* just before its departure for St. Helena. The picture would have an immense success in England.

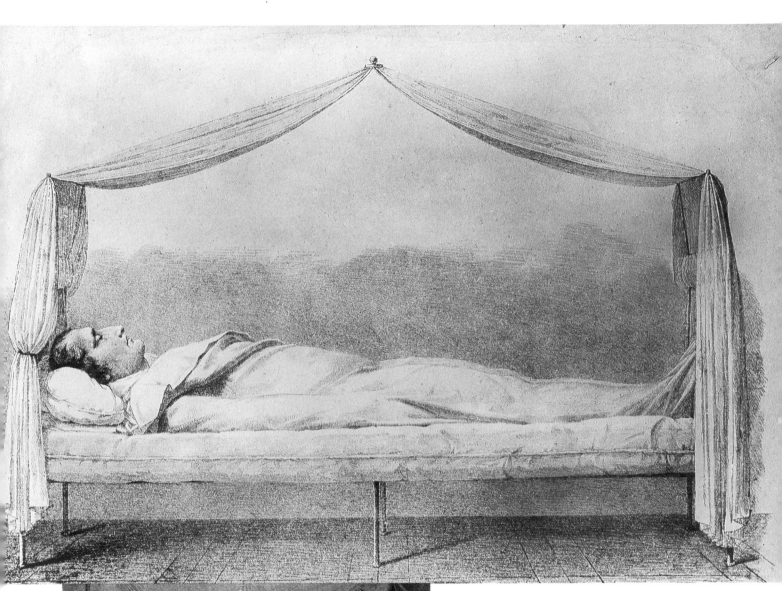

opposite: Joseph Merry Blondel, *Napoleon between the Geniuses of His Destiny*. St. Helena would give the Napoleonic myth its finishing touch. Needless to say, the death of the hero inspired a number of representations, among them the painting seen here.

above: Frederick Marryat, *Napoleon Laid Out on His Austerlitz Camp Bed*, 1821. Fourteen hours after the Emperor died on 5 May 1821 Captain Marryat, on orders from Sir Hudson Lowe, Governor of St. Helena, made the somber drawing that became the prototype for an engraving published in London on 26 July 1821. From the latter came the lithograph seen here.

left: Louis Marchand, *Napoleon Laid Out Following His Death*, 1821. This sketch, made by the Emperor's head valet, offers an interesting comparison with the image limned by Captain Marryat. Here we see the salon at Longwood House, Napoleon's residence on St. Helena, transformed into the bedchamber where the exile died.

above: Anonymous engraving, *The Funeral Cortege of Napoleon I*. The realism of the image stands in marked contrast to the astonishing allegory reproduced on the facing page.

opposite: Jean Alaux, *Napoleon's Tomb in the Vale of Geranium on St. Helena*. The simple tomb bears no inscription, the English unwilling for the title Emperor to appear there. For the vision above, Alaux found a source in Horace Vernet's *Apotheosis of Napoleon*.

overleaf, pages 106–107: Napoleon's last will and testament. 'I desire that my ashes should repose on the banks of the Seine, in the midst of the French people whom I have loved so much.' The document thus ends with a true hero's epitaph. In mid-April 1821, Napoleon dictated his will to

Montholon and then spent five hours copying it so as to make the document incontestable. It is a monument, simultaneously a resumé of an entire life, addressed to posterity, and a vision of the future. To his son, the dying man urged that he 'never do battle, or cause any harm to France.' He also took one last shot at the English, rationalized his defeat, thanked his family, justified the arrest and execution of the Duc d'Enghien, and then went on to parcel out his fortune. It was as if he imagined he could afford his dynasty the advantages that Antony had gained from Caesar's will. Counting the names cited in four codicils, there were no less than 97 legatees meant to benefit, in one degree or another, from the 6 million francs invested at the time of Napoleon's departure from Paris in 1815, plus accumulated interest. The document bears

four seals: the eagle, Napoleon's coat-of-arms, the arms of Montholon and Bertrand respectively, and the cypher of the valet, the last three representing the executors of the will. Attached to the testament was a long and detailed inventory of objects and pieces of linen and clothing. Then, a fortnight before his death, Napoleon dictated another will, this time political and intended for his son. It constituted a veritable program for the 19th century. However, it was the Napoleonic legend and myth that would give the century its true charter, to which the reign of the Emperor served as a prelude.

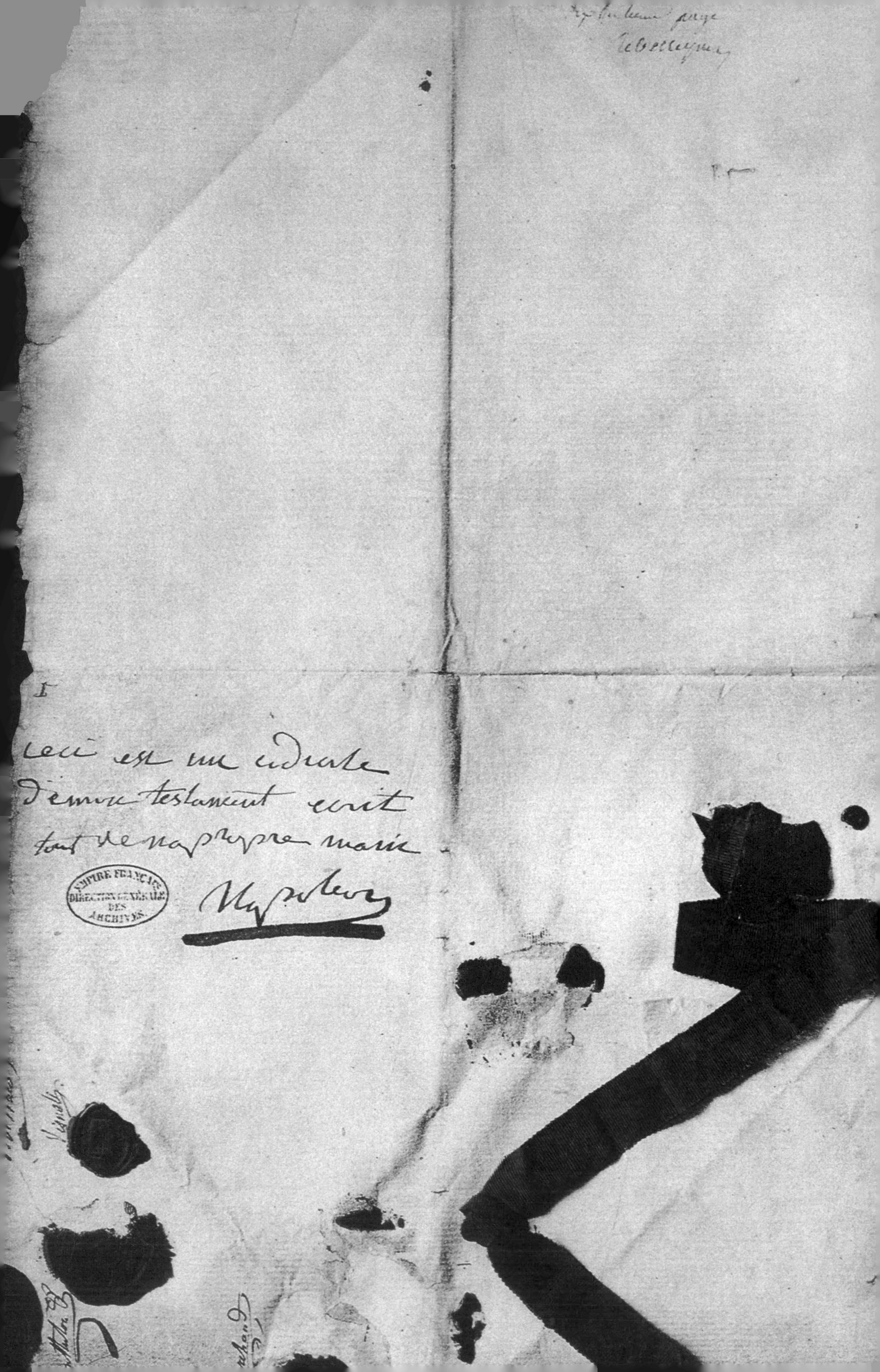

à la bonne page
télégraphie

I

ceci est une indicale
d'mon testament écrit
tout de ma propre main.

Napoléon

EMPIRE FRANÇAIS
DIRECTION GÉNÉRALE
DES
ARCHIVES

avril le 16 1821 Longwood. [illegible]

Ceci est un codicile de mon testament.

1° je désire que mes cendres reposent sur les bords de la Seine au milieu de ce peuple français que j'ai tant aimé

2° je lègue aux comtes Bertrand, Montholon et à Marchand l'argent, bijoux, argenterie, porcelaine, meubles, livres, armes et généralement tout ce qui m'appartient dans l'île de Ste Hélène

Ce codicile tout entier écrit de ma main est signé et scellé de mes armes.

Napoléon

Annexé à la minute d'un acte de dépôt reçu par moi Notaire à Paris soussigné aujourd'hui vingt six mars mil huit cent cinquante trois.

Noël

Signé et paraphé par nous Président du tribunal, selon notre procès verbal de ce jour Paris vingt six mars 1853.

Debelleyme

Visé pour timbre à Paris 2e Bureau le vingt six Mars 1853 [illegible] reçu un franc cinquante centimes & Enregistré le même jour f. 31 [illegible] reçu cinq francs & cinquante centimes [illegible]

1-50
5-50
7-"

[illegible]

Napoleon haunted the whole of the 19th century, as views of him oscillated between naïve fervor on the part of those who remembered him as the people's god and a considered sense that he was the Great Man living out the mysterious ways of Providence. In iconography, he could be seen meditating on destiny, with an eye fixed on the infinite, or, as popular *images d'Épinal* preferred, in a state of apotheosis illuminating the age.

THE GREAT MAN
of the 19th century

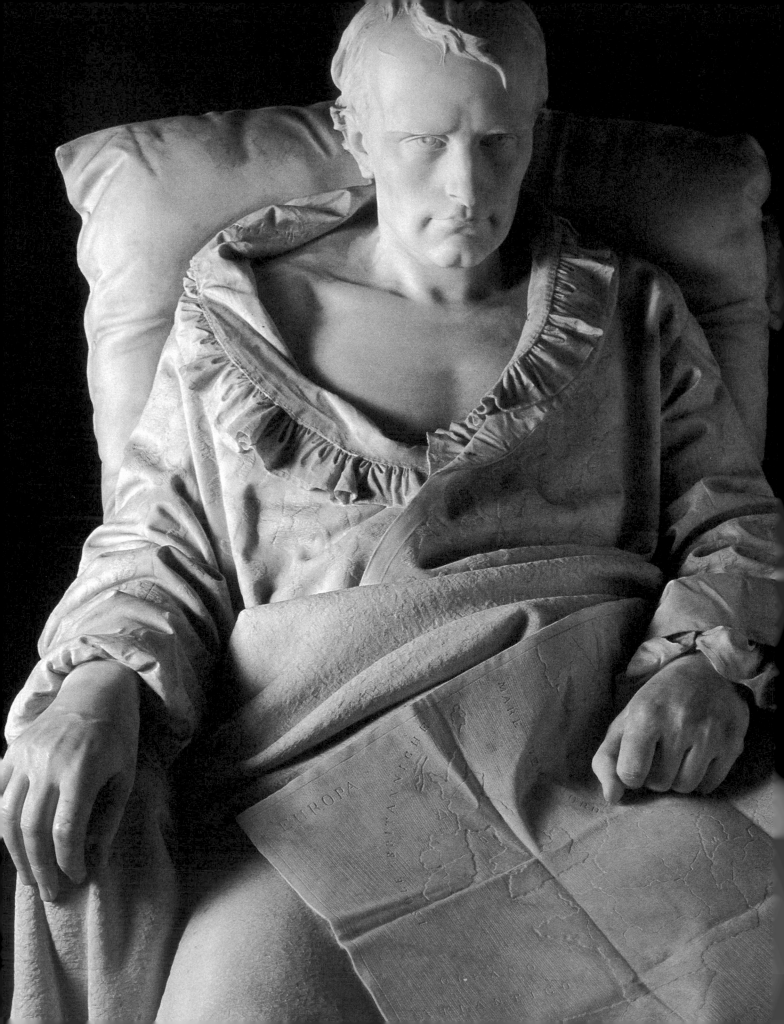

'I AM CALLED

to change the world,' said Napoleon to his brother Joseph. He also changed our capacity to imagine. Like all myths worthy of the name, the Napoleonic myth evolved in the course of time. During the 19th century it renewed itself in successive waves. Slow but decisive, the first wave was set off by missionaries from St. Helena, the authors of a literature which, in the 1950s, would be called 'Helenian,' as if it had derived from Hellenic times. Such writing spread the gospel of Napoleonic martyrdom. After that came Romanticism, which took up the torch, ever more identifying the modern hero and his ideals with the figure of the Emperor. After the revolution of 1830, ending the Bourbon Restoration, the myth truly blossomed, the sole winner perhaps in those momentous days in July. It culminated in 1840, when the return of the ashes left France in possession of the sacred remains. As Romanticism achieved aesthetic and cultural dominance, it shamelessly appropriated the Great Man of History. The Romantics produced a flood of works—literature, painting, sculpture—dealing with Napoleon, his time, and the epic dreams he brought to life. One of the masterpieces that sprang from this Imperial proliferation was François Rude's bronze sculpture *Napoleon Awakening to Immortality*, a monument commissioned by a former captain of the Guard and installed in 1846 at Fixin in Burgundy.

The Second Empire came into effect after the 1848 revolution against the July Monarchy—a revolution that owed little to Napoleonism—and the coup d'état of 2 December 1851. Although a political triumph of Bonapartism, it did nothing to recharge the cult of the new Emperor's uncle, the legend of Napoleon the Great being

opposite: Vincenzo Vela, The *Last Days of Napoleon I*, c.1866. Exhibited at the Universal Exposition of 1867, this marble sculpture counts among the most beautiful art works celebrating the Napoleonic myth.

right: Image d'Épinal, *The Apotheosis of Napoleon I.* Here the anonymous artist places Napoleon in the midst of both his own soldiers and the heroes of past centuries.

APOTHÉOSE DE NAPOLÉON.

an embarrassment for Napoleon the Lesser, as Victor Hugo characterized the two Bonaparte sovereigns. Between 1851 and 1870, a republican counter-myth came into being, both to denounce the regime of Napoleon III and to re-evaluate negatively the place of Napoleon I in the history of France, thus excoriating the link between the First Empire and the Second. After the defeat of 1870, however, the old myth resurfaced, this time becoming a kind of national property, a patriotic reference point for a France humiliated and stripped of Alsace-Lorraine. Now it was possible to be Napoleonian without being Bonapartist, and so the Third Republic, in its turn, annexed the figure of the Great Man, upgraded furthermore to the status of national hero and professor of energy. With an eye firmly fixed on that blue line in the Vosges, France cultivated the memory of the victorious commander. Stung by Germany and the humiliation of Sedan, the French dreamed of Iéna (Jena). In 1921, with Alsace-Lorraine finally back in the French fold, Marshal Foch, victor in the Great War of 1914–1918, stood before the red porphyry tomb in the crypt of the Invalides and paid homage to the sword of Austerlitz.

By then the mythic image of Napoleon had undergone a century of transformations, always keeping pace with the ins and outs of history. A man for all times whom misfortunate never ceases to enlarge, Napoleon understood his situation well when he declared: 'The more I shall be persecuted, the better it shall be for the world.' Little did he fear the historians hostile to his person as well as to his reign, knowing they would be chewing on granite. For the primary causes of his fate, Napoleon looked to Providence, blaming it for everything from the maritime routs to the fires of Moscow and the Russian winter. 'The obstacles that make one fail do not in any way come from men; they come from elements in nature . . . water, air, and fire, all nature and nothing but nature. These are what have been the enemies of a universal regeneration commanded by nature itself. The problems of Providence are insoluble.' Thus, the Little Corporal placed himself under the protection of transcendence much more than under that of history. Just how high would he not aspire?

opposite: Pellerin, *The Defeated Emperor Galvanizing the Troops by His Courage*. The Battle of Waterloo, a fatal defeat for Napoleon, found its way into popular legend. This colored woodcut appears to have been based upon a painting by Steuben entitled *Napoleon at Mont-Saint-Jean*. The commander would also be depicted in the last square of reserve troops heroically outrunning Death. In addition, Raffet published an extraordinary series of lithographs devoted to the tragic day at Waterloo.

above: Horace Vernet, *The Apotheosis of Napoleon*. 1921. The son of Carle, Horace Vernet was involved from the start with the hagiographic canons of the Napoleonic cult. Under the Restoration (1815–1830), his studio became a meeting place for the Eagle's loyalists. In 1822 the studio gained considerable influence after the artist made it an exhibition space for seven of his paintings rejected by the Salon for political reasons. He would become the official painter under Louis-Philippe and then again under Napoleon III.

left: Anonymous caricature, *The Leipzig Barber Shop*. The tradition of mocking Napoleon, which began as early 1796, continued after his fall and throughout the 19th century.

DEATH
and transfiguration

'Had I died on the throne, in the clouds of absolute power, I would have remained a problem for a great many people. Today, thanks to misfortune, every hour strips away my tyrant's skin.' Napoleon understood only too well that his destiny had taken a new turn. Indeed, he had already anticipated its direction. The *Mémorial*, for instance, constantly returns to the same idea—that Napoleon was the heir to the Revolution. Here lay the key to posterity and, above all, the Romantic cult. We have only to read this affirmation: 'Nothing henceforth can destroy or erase the great principles of our Revolution. These grand and beautiful truths should remain for all time! They will be the faith, the religion, the morality of all peoples, and that memorable era will be associated with my person.'

Revolutionary Emperor, organizer of a new Europe, purveyor of dreams and ideals, Napoleon launched the whole of his posthumous career with the publication of the *Mémorial* in 1823. A number of important writers had already recorded their veneration of the fallen hero, among them Heine ('The Two Grenadiers,' a work of 1816 published in 1822), Stendhal (*Napoléon*, also of 1816 but not published until 1929), Byron ('Ode to Napoleon'), and Casimir Delavigne (*Messéniennes*), a writer somewhat forgotten today but a respected figure in his own time. They were the leading edge of what would become a tidal wave. When the announcement of the Emperor's death came, it stirred few emotions in France—at first. Elsewhere

the news had some immediate impact. In Italy, for instance, Manzoni wrote his 'Ode on the 5th of May' ('[A hand from above] led him along the flowering paths of hope where desires subside before infinite Grace, where human glory disappears, sinks into oblivion and the void'). Nonetheless, it was in France that the Eagle would take posthumous flight. In Paris, on 27 October 1821, the actor Talma, Napoleon's old friend, played the Emperor's head in a performance of *Sylla*, a tragedy by Victor-Joseph-Étienne Jouy, he too quite forgotten today.

Towards Romanticism Lamartine ('His coffin is sealed: God has judged him! Silence!: His crime and

right: François Rude, *Napoleon Awakening to Immortality*, 1845–1847, Fixin, Burgundy. Among the Napoleonic works made by Rude, this bonze is without doubt his masterpiece. The unveiling on 19 September 1847 generated great enthusiasm for the cause.

opposite: Oscar Rex, *It Is Finished: Napoleon on St. Helena*, 1857. Along with immortality, exile proved to be an irresistible subject for art works, such as the painting seen here.

The sublime death quite simply blew open doors on every side. How could Louis XVIII, potbellied and gout-ridden as he was, or Charles X, a libertine grown bigoted with age, compete with the man in the little hat? The puffy Napoleon of later years was forgotten, replaced by selective memory, which recalled only the proud young Bonaparte or the Master with the world cradled in his hand, held aloft at the end of a raised arm. Souvenirs of the Revolution, echoes of the epic, red ribbons proudly worn by the elderly, young excited brains—everything conspired to fuel the Napoleonic revival.

If painting lingered somewhat behind, no matter. Actually, Hippolyte Bellangé managed to get his *Battle of Borodino* into the Salon of 1822, even if Horace Vernet, in the same year, had to organize a private exhibition for his *Death of Poniatowski and Montmirail*.

When, following the departure of Charles X, the tricolore flew from the towers of Notre-Dame, everything came tumbling together—Revolution, Empire, Republic, Napoleon. The golden legend had swept up the Little Corporal and banished his dark twin to the marginal world of the narrow-minded. Not for many years would the evil sibling revive. Romanticism adopted Napoleon, his aquiline look, his élan, his immortal brigades. The first and forgettable monuments (no one reads Lebrun or Barthélemy and Méry anymore) gradually gave way to more durable productions. If, as the Austrian writer Franz Grillparzer said, 'the gods could not tolerable their like in him' ('Napoleon,' an ode of 1816), the Pole Adam Mickiewicz would reply: 'God is with Napoleon! Napoleon is with us!' (*Pan Tadeusz* [1834]), while Goethe saluted him for being a 'resumé of the world.' The century belonged to Napoleon Bonaparte. The rise to power of Romanticism's Napoleonic legend diffused the myth far and wide, from 1830 onward. Already, around 1820, a young writer had purchased a bust of Napoleon and glued to the base a bit of paper, which read: 'What he accomplished with the sword, I shall accomplish with the pen.' A few years hence, he would sign his works Honoré de Balzac.

his exploits now weigh in the balance.' ['Bonaparte,' 1822]) and Vigny held fast to their royalist positions, but Victor Hugo, who declaimed 'He passed through glory, he passed through crime / Only to arrive at sorrow' ('Bonaparte,' *Odes et Ballades*), proved almost emblematic in his embrace of Romanticism and its rally round the figure of Napoleon. In 1827, the year of the famous Preface to hia drama *Cromwell*, Hugo published an ode to the Vendôme Column. It was his response to an insult directed at the soldiers of the Grand Army when the Austrian Embassy gave a ball and instructed its butlers not to announce the Marshals of the Empire by their titles.

The change of direction had begun, clearing the way for Napoleon to make his entrance into literature. In 1828 everyone would be warbling Henri Béranger's masterpiece 'Les Souvenirs du peuple' ('It will all be about your glory / Safe under thatch where none fears. / The humble cottage, in fifty years, / Shall hear no other history'). In 1829 Hugo published 'Lui' and thus broke definitively with the Restoration. The seventeen-stanza poem formed part of *Les Orientales*, the first large collection of the new Hugolien Romanticism. As for historians, Baron de Norvins produced his *Histoire de Napoléon et de la Grande Armée* in 1827, truly a vintage year for the Napoleonic cult. This landmark work would go through many editions, notably in 1839 when it appeared with illustrations by Raffet. Among the most paraphrased and illustrated accounts should be cited 'The Nocturnal Review' by the Austrian balladeer Zedlitz (1826).

opposite: François-Joseph Sandmann, *Napoleon on St. Helena*. Overwhelmed by adverse fate, as already seen in the painting by Oscar Rex, Napoleon remains on his feet, facing the ocean from atop his St, Helena rock. The painting, a watercolor, was executed at the request and precise instructions of Louis Marchand, the exiled Emperor's head valet.

above: Nicolas-Eustache Maurin, *Napoleon I Dictating His Memoires*. This favored theme allowed the Great Man to be seen in his last decisive action, passing on to the world the power of his words. Maurin is also known for his painting entitled *The Corporal's Commission at Lodi*, its subject a key episode in the legend.

left: George Cattermole, *Napoleon I Dictating His Memoires*. The dethroned Emperor continues to reign through his words.

opposite: Charles-Auguste-Guillaume Steuben, *Napoleon I Dictating His Memoires to General Gourgaud*, c. 1824. In this painting, Steuben, a pupil of François Gérard, Robert Lefèvre, and Pierre-Paul Prud'hon (himself a leading painter of the legend), realized what would become the most famous representation of the Savior giving birth to the Napoleonic gospel. General Gourgaud had emerged as one of the four Napoleonic evangelists, along with Bertrand, Montholon, and Las Cases. Las Cases had been made General and aide-de-camp to Napoleon immediately after Waterloo.

above: Charles-Auguste-Guillaume Steuben, *Death of Napoleon on St. Helena*, c. 1823. A canonic motif, the death scene at Longwood House caught the interest of numerous painters, among them Steuben, whose preparatory sketch is reproduced here. The final version exists in several copies, including one at the Napoleon Museum in Arenenberg.

above: Horace Vernet, *Napoleon on His Deathbed*, 1825, private collection. In this pious reconstruction, Vernet imagined his dead hero with a rejuvenated, Christ-like face, a laurel crown on his head, and a crucifix on his chest. The portrayal was very much part of the Napoleonic cult, along with such relics as clothing, dentifrice, pencils, toilette articles, and the items seen at right and opposite.

right: A fragment of Napoleon's casket, brought back from St. Helena in 1840 aboard the *Belle-Poule* (private collection).

opposite, above: A lock of Napoleon's hair snipped by General Bertrand on St. Helena (private collection).

opposite, below: A bit of St. Helena earth collected by a pilgrim in 1969 (private collection).

THE 'TRACEABILITY' OF OBJECTS

The historical memento, unlike a work of art, should have a provenance. Among mementos related to the Empire, an object that is not clearly identified must absolutely have 'traceability.' A lock of Napoleon's hair should come from someone close to the Emperor, and the person who received the lock should identify himself and sign a paper to the effect. Finally, the history of the object should be known.

The same procedure applies to all other historical objects. Family tradition is not enough, the authenticity of the information must be provable. The price of an historical object with provenance can be as much as fifteen times that of an object with an attribution that is only approximate. A lock of Napoleon's hair without provenance can range from 300 to 800 euros. With provenance, it could fetch as much as 1,500 or even 10,000 euros. The value depends upon the solidity of the pedigree.

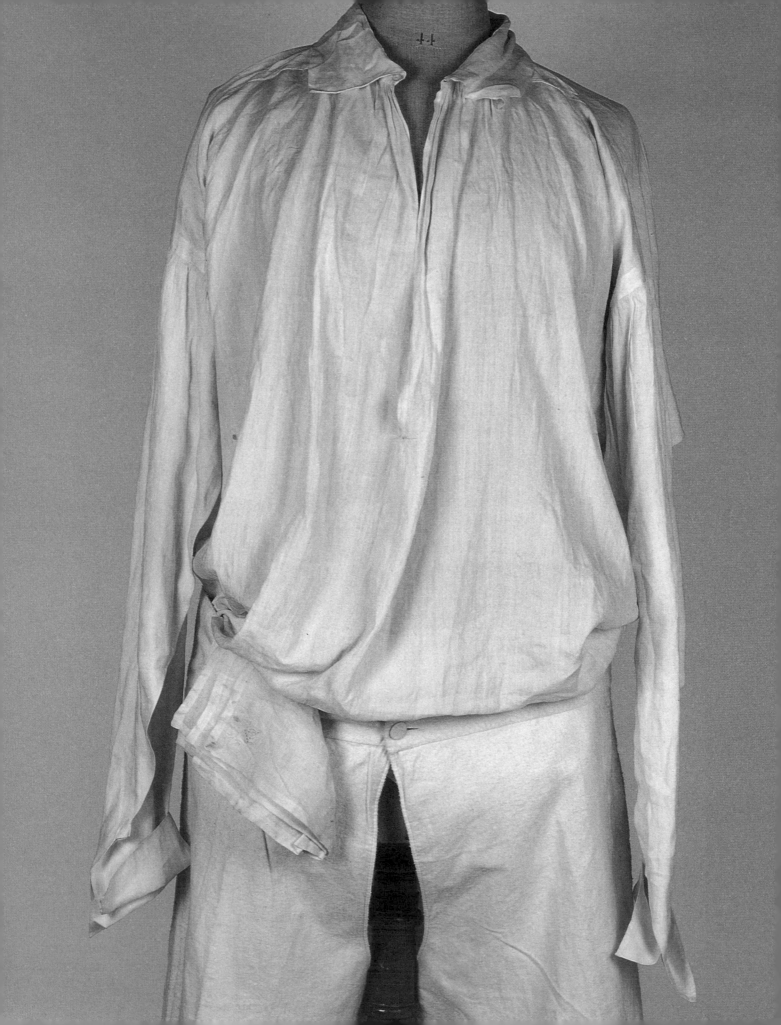

Objets d'art with historical provenance can also fetch ten times the price of similar works lacking solid credentials. A simple goblet made of silver by Biennais (1798–1809) could be priced at around 300–400 euros. The same goblet engraved with the arms of Napoleon I could be worth 20,000–25,000 euros. One should be on guard against false attributions, doubtful pedigrees, and fakes. Knowledge of the period in question is indispensable and can prevent serious mistakes. P.-J.C.

opposite: The last clothing worn by the Emperor on St. Helena (private collection).

above: Princesse de Chimay, *Portrait of Napoleon in Limbo*, 1822, private collection.

right and below: A bottle of dentifrice and a pair of stockings used by Napoleon on St. Helena (private collection).

right and above: Personal items found in Napoleon's gold work-box and left to the city of Paris by General Bertrand in 1840 (private collection).

opposite: Relics of the Emperor given by Chandellier, Napoleon's chef at Longwood House.

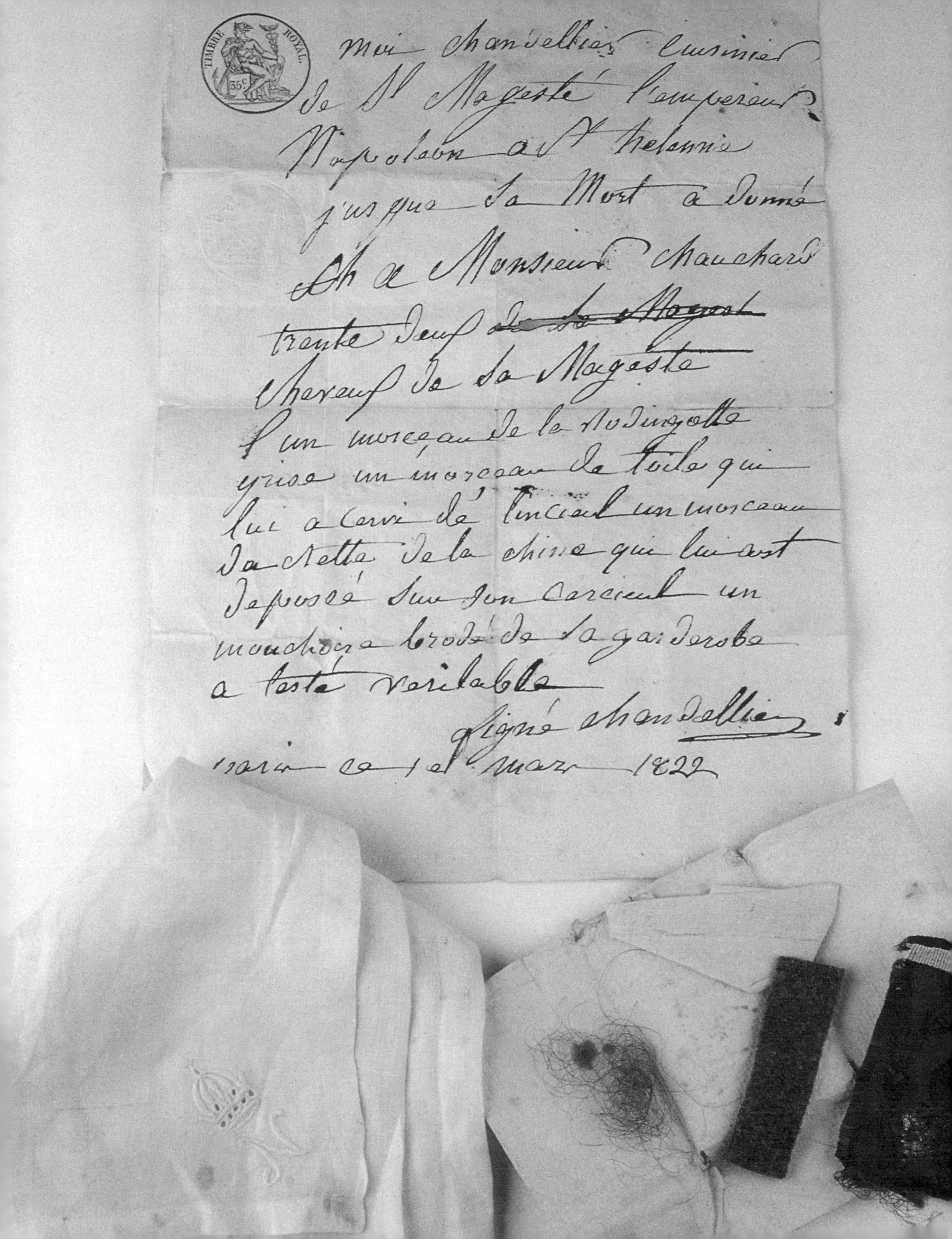

Moi Chandellier cuisinier
de Sa Majesté l'empereur
Napoléon à St hélenne
jusqua sa Mort a donné

Eh à Monsieur Marchand
trente deuf ~~de Sa Majest~~
cheveux de Sa Majesté
f un morceau de le Rodingotte
grise un morceau de toile qui
lui a servi de linciul un morceau
de Nette de la chine qui lui est
deposé sur son cercieul un
mouchoir brodé de Sa garderobe
a testé veritable

signé Chandellier
paris ce 1er mars 1822

The library of that insatiable reader, Napoleon, contained some 60,000 volumes. Most of the collection has disappeared, owing primarily to the fires at the Château de Saint-Cloud and the Tuileries. On St. Helena the Emperor imported approximately 2,500 books.

right: Books and maps, bound in red morocco, from Napoleon's library (private collection).

below: A copy of Josephine's *Mémoires* received by Napoleon several weeks before his death (private collection).

below, center: Roman history, bedside reading for the Emperor: Rollin's *Histoire romaine depuis la fondation de Rome jusqu'à la fin de la République*, the section on Hannibal's armies crossing the Alps well annotated

far right: The English grammar studied by the Emperor at Longwood House.

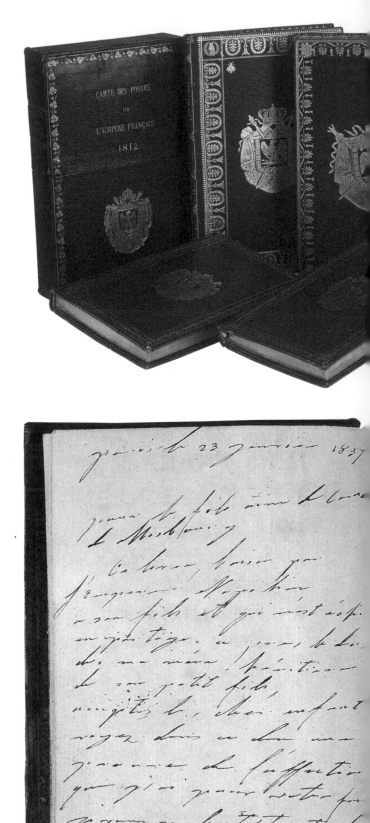

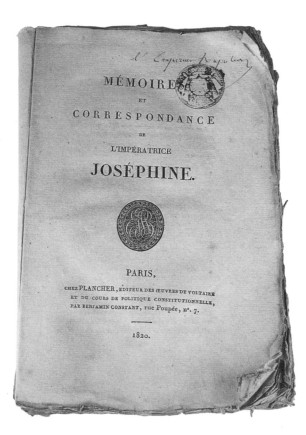

HISTOIRE
ROMAINE
DEPUIS LA FONDATION
DE ROME
jusqu'à la fin de la
REPUBLIQUE
PAR MONSR. ROLLIN

Ancien Recteur de l'Université de Paris, Professeur d'Eloquence au Collége Royal, & Associé à l'Académie Royale des Inscriptions & Belles - Lettres.

TOME QUATRIEME.

A LEIDE,
Chez J. DE WETSTEIN & FILS.
MDCCLXXII.

Napoleon
from E.V.Holland
by Lord Bathursts permission

THE NAPOLEON
of the Romantics

*It was here [Ajaccio],
the new Rome,
That on the day
of the Assumption
Once more God
became man.
Napoleon! Napoleon!*
Costa de Baselica,
L'Ajaccienne (1848)

'I belong to that generation which, born with the century and nourished on the Emperor's bulletins, always had before them an unsheathed sword, only to arrive ready to seize it just when France resheathed it, this time in the scabbard of the Bourbons' (Alfred de Vigny, *Servitude et Grandeur militaires* [1835]). 'One man alone was then alive in Europe; everyone else tried to fill their lungs with the air he had breathed. Every year France made him a gift of three hundred thousand young men; and, with a smile, he took this new fiber pulled from the heart of humanity, twisted it in his hands, and made a new string for his bow; he then took one of his arrows and sent it flying across the world, until it fell into a vale on a deserted island under a weeping willow' (Alfred de Musset, *The Confessions of a Child of a Century* [1836]). Quotations of this sort could go on and on. Romantic literature, dominant throughout the July Monarchy (1830–1848), plumbed the Napoleonic theme to its very depths. In 1830 Stendhal published *The Red and the Black*, the first great Napoleonic novel, in which Julien Sorel read and reread the *Mémorial*, that bible of the century, imagining that it could be a model for his own life: 'Julien, standing on his big rock, looked at the sky, basking in the August sun. Cicadas sang in the field below the rock; when they quit silence suddenly reigned on every side. At his feet he could see the countryside for miles around. Several sparrow hawks took flight from the boulders above him, catching his attention from time to time as they quietly circled in wide arcs. Rather mechanically, Julien let his eye follow the bird of prey, struck by its calm but powerful movements. He envied that force; he envied that isolation. This was the fate of Napoleon; would it one day be his?' (*Le Rouge et le noir*).

A hero fit for novels In both name and memory, the Emperor haunted the world of fiction. Three

above: Jean-Auguste-Dominique Ingres, *Study for the Apotheosis of Napoleon I*, 1853. Romantic iconography outdid even that of the Empire. For the ceiling above the Emperor's Salon at the Hôtel de Ville in Paris, Ingres painted an heroically nude Napoleon treated *di sotto in sù*—that is, in steep perspective viewed from below. This fantasy disappeared in the fire set by the Communards in 1871, but a sense of it survives in the study reproduced here. The Latin inscription reads: *In nepote redivivus*, meaning that Napoleon I survived in his nephew, Napoleon III, whose government had commissioned the painting.

opposite: Félix-Henri-Emmanuel Philippoteaux, *Bonaparte at the Battle of Rivoli*, 1844. In this depiction of a famous battle the Consul watches the frantic withdrawal of an Austrian column. Beginning in 1804, painters of battle scenes focused more and more on the commander, especially under the Empire. The tendency attained its perfection in the work seen here.

years after *The Red and the Black*, young Honoré de Balzac brought out *The Country Doctor* (*Le Médecin de campagne*), in which Goguelat, the old soldier, expounds at length upon the popular Napoleonic legend and its development. The theatre as well placed Napoleon at stage center. Countless history plays came before the public, generally as re-enactments of one episode or another in the epic story. A characteristic piece was Alexandre Dumas's *Napoleon Bonaparte or Thirty Years of the History of France*, which opened in 1831. A year earlier, in a play about the adolescent Bonaparte enrolled at the Brienne military academy, the actress Virginie Déjazet put on a cadet's uniform and played the leading role *en travesti*. And she would do it again in 1867! Among the plays with high poetic ambition, a prime example would be Edgar Quinet's *Napoléon* (1836), a work obsessed with the singular man, the hero. Sacrificed, a victim of destiny and his own excesses, this Napoleon, like Prometheus, emerges as the demiurge, a vital force giving rise to a new era. True enough, the historical Napoleon gobbled up an entire generation, but he also led the way in the development of human individuality.

The epic Napoleon also dominated poetry, as a prestigious figure, a unique and solitary genius, whose isolation appeared to be the rule 'even in the realm of the imagination.' He quite simply consisted

widespread devotion to Napoleon among the peasantry: 'I have noted most often in the cottages of peasants representations of the Emperor visiting the pesthouse in Jaffa but also on his deathbed on St. Helena. These two images bear a striking resemblance to the images of saints in the Christian religion. In one, Napoleon appears like a savior who heals the plague-stricken by touching them; in the other, he dies a death of expiation.'

Paintings of the legend Horace Vernet, who made his debut at the Salon of 1812 with a painting entitled *The Capture of an Entrenched Camp*, fixed the pictorial rules for an entire generation of artists dedicated to the legend and its promotion. Bouhot, Couder, Hersent, Langlois, Lecomte, Lejeune, Meyer, Rouget, Steuben, Yvon—these artists, born between 1780 and 1800, would breathe new life into the Napoleonic story. Their works are everywhere at Versailles, the very temple of such production. Paul Delaroche, a more significant artist, took up the legend only from time to time, and not before 1838, when he painted a portrait of the master in his study. In 1845, however, he exhibited one of the century's most memorable canvases, a portrait of the dejected Emperor slumped in a chair at Fontainebleau following his first abdication. Poignant, dramatic, and grand, even if unflattering, this view of Napoleon at the turning point in his life captures both the mortal man overwhelmed by circumstances and the hero taking account of the reverses imposed upon him by fate, a fate that has yet to defeat him. The past, the present, and the future all seem to be reflected at once in his somber, brooding look. Moved by the painting, Barbey d'Aurevilly wrote: 'The face of the Emperor is sublime with suffering, and it is human . . . , it is neither the face of an Ajax nor that of a Prometheus. Rather, it is the face of the most intelligent of men, who senses that his genius is not dead, even if he is defeated.'

of all the images and representations the people made of him. Music too felt the Romantic pull of Napoleon, an example being Berlioz's 1834 cantata entitled *The Fifth of May* or *The Death of Napoleon*.

For present purposes, however, let us consider painting and lithography, at a moment when the Horace Vernets, the Delaroches, the Charlets, and the Raffets were coming to the fore. Nicolas-Toussaint Charlet exhibited *The Grenadier of Waterloo* in 1817 and then made history in 1836 with his *Episode from the Russian Campaign*. Denis-Auguste-Marie Raffet specialized in pious depictions of Napoleon on bivouac or the Emperor drying his boots before a cottage hearth. Popular engravings known as *images d'Épinal* disseminated, by the tens of thousands, portraits of the Emperor, the Marshals, l'Aiglon, battles scenes, the farewells at Fontaine-bleau, St. Helena, the deathbed, etc. Heinrich Heine, in *Conditions in France* (1833), commented on the

above: J.P.M. Jazet (after Horace Vernet), *Napoleon Rising from the Tomb*, 1840. In this canvas, painted in the year the ashes were returned, Jazet appears to have gathered up all the codes of Romantic representation and recast them in hyperbolic terms.

opposite: Jean-Baptiste Mauzaisse, *Napoleon I, Crowned by Time, Writing the Civil Code*, Salon 1833. This allegorical work, with its reference to legislation, typifies the kind of glorification encouraged by Louis-Philippe. Among the dense array of symbols are Time's scythe, now abandoned, and Napoleon posed like Moses engraving the Tablets of Law.

The return of the ashes Even the republicans lauded the great man, leaving only the legitimatists to disdain the Romantic wave of adulation. Louis-Philippe, cleverly enough, decided to appropriate the cult and turn it to his own advantage. With nothing to fear from an Aiglon dying at Schönbrunn, and with the aging Marshals rallying to his side (Soult and Mortier were even ministers), the King arranged to have the ashes returned to France in 1840. With this, the Napoleonic legend realized its apotheosis and France a moment of national unity. Already in October 1830 Auguste Anicet-Bourgeois had made the longed-for consecration the dénouement of his play *Napoléon*. In 1822, shortly after the Emperor

died, Montholon had requested it. In petitions and poems alike (Hugo, the writing duo Barthélemy and Méry, etc.), the demand grew increasingly urgent, despite a few dissenting voices, like that of Auguste Barbier, who answered Hugo in his poem 'L'Idole' (1831): 'Again Napoleon! Again his great image! / How this rude warrior astride his sorrel / Has cost us blood and tears and outrage! / For a few leafy branches of laurel!' Still, France wanted back its god. With the return of the ashes in 1840, the Romantics had their Napoleonic triumph, a victory shared by another Bonaparte. A year earlier, Louis Napoleon, patiently awaiting his moment, had published *The Napoleonic Idea*, in which he hailed the 'plebeian hero,

who assured the independence of all peoples and who was the true representative of our revolution.' Victor Hugo, again, welcomed the Emperor, if only in death: 'Sire, you shall return borne high on a car / Glorious, crowned, sanctified like Charlemagne / And great like Caesar!' The idol of soldiers, the hero, the Emperor, the French god had rejoined his own. In England Thomas Carlyle summed it up thus: 'He had to sink there, mournfully as a man seldom did; and break his great heart, and die,—this poor Napoleon; a great implement too soon wasted, till it was useless; our last Great Man!' (On *Heroes and Hero Worship* [1841]). Also in 1840, on the 3rd of June, Victor Hugo, elected to the French Academy, included these remarks in his reception address:

At the beginning of this century, France was a magnificent spectacle in the eyes of all nations. A man then took over and made her so huge that she encompassed all of Europe. This man come from the shadows had arrived in a mere few years at a degree of royalty perhaps never seen before in startled history. A revolution had given birth to him, a people had chosen him, a pope had crowned him. Every year he rolled back the frontiers of his Empire . . . . He had effaced the Alps like Charlemagne and the Pyrenees like Louis XIV. He had built his State at the center of Europe like a citadel, providing it with the bastions and outer fortifications of ten monarchies that he had brought into his Empire and into his family. Everything about this man was large-scaled and splendid. He rose above Europe like an extraordinary vision.

The liberator of peoples The image of Napoleon may be etched in blood on the martyrologue of those European nations made to suffer because of him, as in Spain during the hideous war that ground on there from 1807 to 1814. Yet where the people identified his endeavors with their own destiny, the Romantic Napoleon rested comfortably in the local pantheon. The great awakening of nationalities— even if in literature only, as it often was—would evolve into a mass phenomenon.

The Holy Alliance, once the enemy of Napoleon and a welcome defense against him, would become the enemy of the peoples. Nationalists and liberals alike saw in Napoleon a defender of the oppressed, a liberator brought down by powerful reactionaries, a propagator of modern ideals. Napoleon, the Genius of liberty. By 1830 the metamorphosis had been achieved. The shadow of the little hat fell over the Europe of nationalities.

At the time of the Italian campaign, Napoleon had managed to find, in several countries taken over by Directory France, writers willing to laud a Bonaparte

MÉMORIAL

DE Sᵗᵉ-HÉLÈNE,

OU

JOURNAL dans lequel se trouve consigné, jour par jour, tout ce qu'a dit et fait NAPOLÉON durant 18 mois;

PAR LE COMTE DE LAS CASES;

Huit vol. in-8°, ou in-12.

CET OUVRAGE SERA ENRICHI D'UNE CARTE TRÈS-DÉTAILLÉE DE SAINTE-HÉLÈNE, ET DU PLAN DE LONGWOOD.

—————

PROSPECTUS.

—————

Nous n'avons pas cru pouvoir faire un meilleur Prospectus pour donner une juste idée de cet Ouvrage précieux sous bien des rapports, et si attendu, que d'en publier la Préface, que nous venons d'obtenir de M. le comte DE LAS CASES.

PRÉFACE.

Les circonstances les plus extraordinaires m'ont tenu long-temps auprès de l'homme le plus extraordinaire que présentent les siècles.

L'admiration me le fit suivre sans le connaître, l'amour m'eût fixé pour jamais près de lui dès que je l'eus connu.

opposite: Horace Vernet, *The Battle of Friedland*, c. 1840. The Romantic era produced a flood of battle paintings, the better to fill the Hall of Battles in Louis-Philippe's new Historical Museum at Versailles.

left: Emmanuel-Joseph de Las Cases, *Mémorial de Sainte-Hélène* (title page), 1823. Even more than images, texts enflamed the Romantic imagination, especially the text of the *Mémorial*. A true memorial site, in the modern sense of the word, this publication, so rich in epic, tragedy, drama, and fiction, rang the bell announcing that a literary revolution had begun. It provided a veritable matrix for all that was to come.

as the embodiment of revolution and liberty, even if it meant a quick change of political horses. Thus in 1797 Ugo Roscolo produced the celebratory *Bonaparte liberatore*. Five years later, however, the same writer would sing a different tune in his *Ultime lettere di Jacopo Ortis*: 'Nature created him a tyrant; the tyrant does not think of his country; he has none.' Under the Empire the hatred aroused by Napoleon turned all of Europe against him. E.M. Arndt, in his *Catechism for the Teutonic Soldier and Warrior* (1813), speaks of a 'monster' from hell, a 'blood-stained horror' with a 'name cursed by widows and orphans.' The Russian Glinka evoked a Satan 'ringed about by death, devastation, and flames.' Too, we have only to recall the paintings of Francisco Goya.

Still, around 1820 and throughout the following decades, much of Europe seemed to forget that it had been occupied more than liberated. From Spain even, where one spoke of *el gran hombre*, to Russia, from Egypt, with its memory of Sultan Abu

Napartuk, to the descendants of the Incas, who considered him a demi-god, his name commanded respect, admiration, veneration. Indeed, numerous writers of every cultural stripe—Austrian, Hungarian, German, English, Russian, Italian, Norwegian—participated fully in the movement or at least felt its vibrations.

The European bards Heinrich Heine had already blazed the trail in 1816 when he published his 'Two Grenadiers,' later set to music by Robert Schumann:

> But I beg you, brother, if by chance
>   You soon shall see me dying,
> Then take my corpse with you back to France,—
>   Let it ever in France be lying.
> The cross of honor with crimson hand
>   Shall rest on my heart as it bound me;
> Give me my musket, in my hand,
>   And buckle my sword around me.
> And there I shall be and listen still,

> In my sentry-coffin staying,
>   Till I feel this thundering cannon's thrill,
>   And horses trampling and neighing.
>   Then my Emperor will ride, well over my grave,
>   Mid sabers bright and smiting;
>   And I'll rise all weaponed up out of my grave,—
>   For the Emperor, the Empeor fighting.

There was also Italy's Alessandro Manzoni, who in the ode 'Il cinque Maggio' ('Fifth of May' [1821]), inspired by Napoleon's death, had introduced into European Romanticism the theme of the chain-bound and martyred Prometheus, combining it with a religious theme:

> He disappeared; his years on a rock over;
> His hangmen ceased their endless, cruel endeavor;
> Trapped in idleness, he saw himself by turns
> An object of bottomless hatred and everlasting regret,
> Or memorable food none can forget
> Of love that forever burns. . . .
> God who strikes down and reverses or raises up and consoles,
> Envelopes him in aureoles
> And brings him close. . . .

In 'All'anno 1830' Gabriele Rossetti, father of the Pre-Raphaelite poet and painter, characterized 'the great soul who dazzled the world' as a 'flash of Italian sunlight.' Meanwhile, in that same year, Poles rose up against their Russian, Prussian, and Austrian overlords, ever mindful that Napoleon had set them free in a buffer state known as the Grand Duchy of Warsaw (1807–1813). André Towianski and Adam Mickiewicz saw the Emperor as a divine messenger sent to re-establish the laws of religion on earth but then abandoned by God for having failed in his mission, whence came Waterloo. Towianski imagined a Poland guided by 'the Spirit of Napoleon,' if only it could re-emerge in a similarly messianic figure. In 'The Year 1812' Mickiewicz cited what he viewed as the climactic year, an opinion he would restate in *Pan Tadeusz*, published in 1834: 'Beautiful year, which found you among us, lingers ever in cherished remembrance / For the people you are the time of verdant abundance / For the soldier "the year of war," and the old folk who adore you / A thing of wonder: In popular song you reign there too.'

The modern man

In 19th-century America, Napoleon was generally admired, thanks to Ralph Waldo Emerson, the transcendentalist poet/philosopher, who proposed that the fallen Emperor be understood as a representative of the democratic classes, a superman bringing to pass everyone's dreams: 'Napoleon is absolutely modern. . . . Bonaparte was the idol of common man because he had in transcendent degree the qualities and powers of common men.' A bit later Friedrich Nietzsche, in *Die fröhliche Wissenschaft* (*The Gay Science* [1882]), analyzed the strong man, the 'natural aristocrat,' the great European continuator of the Renaissance. The Nietzschean version of 'superman Napoleon' would captivate the whole of the 20th century: 'To him therefore will come one day the honor of having re-created in Europe a world in which man will prevail over the tradesman and the philistine, perhaps even over "woman" cajoled as she is by christianism, by the fanciful spirit of the 18th century, and most of all by the "modern idea." Napoleon, who lives in this idea and, generally, in civilization itself, both of them personal enemies of a sort, affirms himself by that very hostility as one of the great perpetuators of the Renaissance. He brought to light one entire face of the antique world, and the most important perhaps, the face of granite. Moreover, who knows whether this element of the antique soul will not one day again master the nationalistic movements so that they too continue to inherit, this time in a positive sense, the work of Napoleon; that Napoleon who wanted, as is known, a Europe all of a piece and that Europe master of the world?'

> Angel or demon! thou,—whether of light
>   The minister, or drkness—still dost sway
> This age of ours; thine eagle's soaring flight
>   Bears us, all breathless, after it away.
>   The eye that from thy presence fain would stray
> Shuns thee in vain; thy mighty shadow thrown
>   Rests on all pictures of the living day.
> And on the threshold of our time alone,
>   Dazzling. yet sombre, stands thy form, Napoleon.
>   Victor Hugo, 'Lui/Him' (1828)

opposite: Paul Delaroche, *Napoleon I at Fontainebleau Following the First Abdication, 6 April 1814*, 1840–1845. One of the century's most remarkable portraits of the Emperor, this visionary image may have been based upon one or more precedents, among them Raffet's *La Pensée*; a scene drawn by Loutrel (after Vernet) as an illustration for Laurent de L'Ardèche's *L'Histoire de l'Empereur Napoléon* (1839). which shows the Emperor seated apart while rereading his act of abdication; and an 1812 engraving by Burdin (after Raffet) entitled simply *Napoléon*. Delaroche's canvas would have immense and lasting success.

Him (Parts I and III)
VICTOR HUGO ('Lui,' December 1828)

I

Above all others, everywhere I see
   His image cold or burning!
My brain it thrills, and oftentime sets free
   The thoughts within me yearning.
My quivering lips pour forth the words
   That cluster in his name of glory —
The star gigantic with its rays of swords
   Whose gleams irradiate all modern story.

I see his finger pointing where the shell
   Should fall to slay most rabble,
And save foul regicides; or strike the knell
   Of weaklings 'mid the tribunes' babble.
A Consul then, o'er young but proud,
   With midnight poring thinned, and sallow,
But dreams of Empire pierce the transient cloud,
   And round pale face and lank locks form the halo.

And soon the Caesar, with an eye a-flame
   Whole nations' contact urging
To gain his soldiers gold and fame!
   Oh, Sun on high emerging,
Whose dazzling lustre fired the hells
   Embosomed in grim bronze, which, free, arose
To change five hundred thousand base-born Tells,
   Into his host of half-a-million heroes!

What! next a captive? Yea, and caged apart,
   No weight of arms enfolded
Can crush the turmoil in that seething heart
   Which Nature — not her journeyman — self-moulded.
Let sordid jailers vex their prize;
   But only bends that brow to lightning,
As gazing from the seaward rock, his sighs
   Cleave though the storm, and haste where France
   looms bright'ning.

Alone, but greater! Broke the sceptre, true!
   Yet lingers still some power—
In tears of woe man's metal may renew
   The temper of high hour;
For, bating breath, o'er list the kings:
   The pinions clipped may grow! the Eagle
May burst, in frantic thirst for home, the rings
   And rend the Bulldog, Fox, and Bear, and Beagle!

And, lastly, grandest! 'tween dark sea and here
   Eternal brightness coming!
The eye so weary's freshened with a tear
   As rises distant drumming
And wailing cheer — they pass the pale:
   His army mourns, though still's the end hid;
And from his war-stained cloak, he answers, 'Hail!'
   And spurns the bed of gloom for throne aye splendid!

(translated by H.L. Williams)

III

Angel, or demon! thou — whether of light
   The minister, or darkness — still dost sway
This age of ours; thine eagle's soaring flight
   Bears us, all breathless, after it away.
   The eye that from thy presence fain would stray
Shuns thee in vain; thy mighty shadow thrown
   Rests on all pictures of the living day,
And on the threshold of our time alone,
Dazzling, yet sombre, stands thy form, Napoleon!

Charles-Auguste-Guillaume Steuben, *The Eight Stages in the Life of Napoleon*, 1826. The old story, this time told, with wit and charm, through the master's 'little hats'! In battle Napoleon kept the 'wings' of his hat turned up parallel with his shoulders, while grenadier officers, both infantry and cavalry, wore their hats in 'column' form, that is, the wings perpendicular, or a right angles, to the shoulders. One of the hats preferred by Napoleon was placed in his coffin.

Thus, when the admiring stranger's steps explore
    The subject-lands that 'neath Vesuvius be,
Whether he wind along the enchanting shore
    To Portici from fair Parthenope,
    Or, lingering long in dreamy reverie,
O'er loveliest Ischia's od'rous isle he stray,
    Wooed by whose breath the soft and am'rous sea
Seems like some languishing sultana's lay, –
A voice for very sweets that scarce can win its way;

Him, whether Paestum's solemn fane detain,
    Shrouding his soul with meditation's power;
Or at Pozzuloli, to the sprightly strain
    Of tarantella danced 'neath Tuscan tower,
    Listening, he while away the evening hour;
Or wake the echoes, mournful, lone and deep,
    Of that sad city, in its dreaming bower
By the volcano seized, where mansions keep
The likeness which they wore at that last fatal sleep;

Or be his bark at Posillippo laid,
    While as the swarthy boatman at his side
Chants Tasso's lays to Virgil's pleased shade, –
    Ever he sees, throughout that circuit wide,
    From shaded nook or sunny lawn espied,
From rocky headland viewed, or flow'ry shore,
    From sea and spreading mead alike descried,
The Giant Mount, tow'ring all objects o'er,
And black'ning with its breath th' horizon evermore!

(19th century translation
of the last four stanzas of Part III)

above: Horace Vernet, *The Battle of Wagram*, Salon 1836. After Carle Vernet and Antoine-Jean Gros, and at the same time as Hippolyte Bellangé, Horace Vernet presented the world with his own painstaking reconstruction of the eponymous battle. At the center of the picture is Napoleon using a spy-glass to observe the impact of the artillery bombardment ordered by General Lauriston, while simultaneously handing a document to a staff officer. In the near background the wounded Bessières has fallen from his horse.

opposite: Adolphe Roehn, *Napoleon Bivouacking on the Eve of Wagram, 5–6 July 1809*, Salon 1810. Scarcely had the battle ended when Roehn gave the Napoleonic legend one of its most characteristic images. Ironically, the scene never took place, since Napoleon remained in conference with his corps commanders until one in the morning and then kept Davout until dawn. He had no rest until the 6th of July at three in the afternoon, taken under a pyramid of drums piled up to shelter him from the sun. The dozing leader, seated in a familiar, canonic pose and back-lit by a blazing campfire, is watched by his Mameluks stretched out on the ground and several Marshals, their faces full of deep thought, indeed veneration. The painting has been seen as an inverted version of Jesus's night on the Mount of Olives.

At night, round the hour of twelve, a crippled
drummer rises from his tomb, makes the rounds with
his tabour, back and forth at an eager pace. The bony
hands rattle away with both drumsticks. Thus does
he beat more than one good drum roll, sounding
many a reveille and many a retreat. The drum
reverberates with strange sounds, marvelous in their
muffled power. They waken the soldiers, long dead in
their graves. Those who, far to the north, remain
buried under frozen snow, and those who lie in Italy,
where the earth they find too hot. And those covered
by the silt of the Nile or the burning sands of
Arabia. All spring from their graves and seize their
arms.

And round the twelfth hour, the trumpeter from
his sepulcher comes forth, blows a muted clarion
call, and arrives on his rearing steed. Then appear all
the long-dead cavalry astride their spectral
chargers—the old squadrons, bloodied but fully
armed in diverse ways. Their white heads gleam
under ghostly helmets, their long swords held high,
grasped by skeletal hands.

And round the hour of twelfth, the commanding
general at last from his tomb emerges. Slowly he
arrives on a white horse, aides-de-camp in full
surround. He wears a little hat and a uniform free of
ornament, a sword hanging at his side. Over the vast
plain the moon spreads a sheet of cold, pale light.
The man in the little hat reviews the troops, the
ranks presenting arms as he rides past. Next the
tattered army moves off and files out, led by fife and
drum.

The marshals and the generals come nigh,
forming a ring about him. The commanding general
of all whispers a single word in the ear of the one
closest by. The word takes flight, making the rounds
from mouth to mouth, all the way soon to the ranks
most distant. The war cry is *France!* The rallying cry:
St. Helena! 'Tis the grand funeral review along the
Champs-Élysées that the deceased Emperor passes,
round the hour of twelve at night.

Zedlitz (1790–1862), *The Nocturnal Review*

above: Denis-Auguste-Marie Raffet, *Napoleon Reviewing
the Guard*, c. 1848, lithograph. With his drawings and
lithographs, Raffet assured a place in the pantheon of
Napoleonic imagery for the guardsmen and common
soldiers serving under the Empire. In another work,
entitled *Grand Review or the Night of 5 May* (1848), Raffet
illustrated the Zedlitz ballad reprinted at left in an English
adaptation.

above: Horace Vernet, *Marshal Moncey and His Troops Defending Paris at the Barrière de Clichy on 30 March 1814*. In 1820 Vernet took up the subject of the French resistance to invasion, thereby identifying patriotism with Napoleonism. The painting seen here glorified Marshal Moncey and, by implication, the grandeur of Imperial France. It is worth noting that Carle and Horace Vernet joined the resistance as citizen soldiers, as did Charlet. The two Vernets are even present in the painting above, right at the side of Marshal Moncey.

opposite: Nicolas-Toussaint Charlet, *Napoleon Bidding Farewell to the Imperial Guard at Fontainebleau, 20 April 1814*, 1825. This is undoubtedly the artist's best-known work, which shows General Petit embracing the Emperor, a grenadier hiding his tears, and, at the left, the four representatives of the Allied Powers. Also present are Bertrand, Drouot, and Gourgaud, but none of the Marshals. Immediately after this emotional scene, Napoleon entered his carriage and passed into legend. On the same day, according to his *Mémoires*, a future emperor of letters took the name by which he would become famous. Instead of Alexandre Davy de la Pailletterie, he chose to be known as Alexandre Dumas.

below: Morin, *Opening the Coffin*, color lithograph. The return of the ashes, around which the official cult and the popular cult, the Romantic Napoleon and the nationalist Napoleon all rallied, marked the culminating point of the Napoleonic myth. Every episode along the way would be illustrated.

right: Eugène Isabey, *Lowering the Coffin onto the* Belle-Poule, *15 October 1840*. The artist was the son of Jean-Baptiste Isabey.

bottom: Anonymous, *Napoleon's Coffin on Board the* Belle-Poule, lithograph. During the voyage from St. Helena to Cherbourg, the catafalque remained on the rear deck, the latter fitted out like a mortuary chapel.

pages 144–145: Facing pages from the *Belle-Poule*'s log (private collection). This copy belonged to Grand Marshal Bertrand.

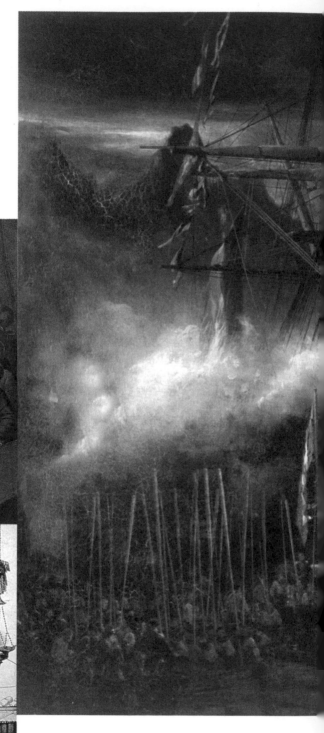

page 148: French officials, such as the Mayor of Saint-Denis, issued numerous announcements related to the state funeral planned for the Emperor.

page 149: Adam Bichebois, *The Emperor's Funeral Procession Passing through the Arc de Triomphe.* The cortege continued all the way to the Invalides on the left bank of the Seine.

page 150, above: Dumouza, *The Catafalque-Boat Coming Alongside the Quay in front of the Invalides*, lithograph.

page 150, below: In this contemporary lithograph the Emperor's remains have arrived under the high dome of the Invalides Church, soon to be known as the 'Saint-Denis of the Bonapartes,' as Jean Tulard

put it. To the strains of a funeral march, Joinville prepares to present the body to King Louis-Philippe.

page 151: Napoleon's tomb was created by Visconti with the assistance of Pradier, Simart, and Jouffroy. The crypt is open to view, allowing the red-porphyry sarcophagus to be seen at all times.

Itinéraire du voyage à Ste Hélène

frégate la Belle Poule.

Départ de la Rade de Toulon.	le 7 Juillet à 6½ du Soir
Arrivée sur la Rade de Cadix.	le 16 Juillet à 7½ du Mat
Départ de la Rade de Cadix.	le 21 Juillet à 6¼ ma
Arrivée sur la Rade de Funchall.	le 24 Juillet 7¾
Départ de la Rade de Funchall.	le 26 Juillet 7h m
Arrivée sur Rade de Sainte Croix.	le 27 Juillet 6h
Départ de la Rade de Sainte Croix.	le 2 août 2h
Arrivée sur Rade de Bahia.	le 28 août 7
Départ de la Rade de Bahia.	le 14 Septem
Arrivée sur Rade de Sainte-Hélène.	le 8 octobre
Départ de la Rade de Sainte hélène.	le 18 oct
Arrivée sur Rade de Cherbourg.	le 30 n

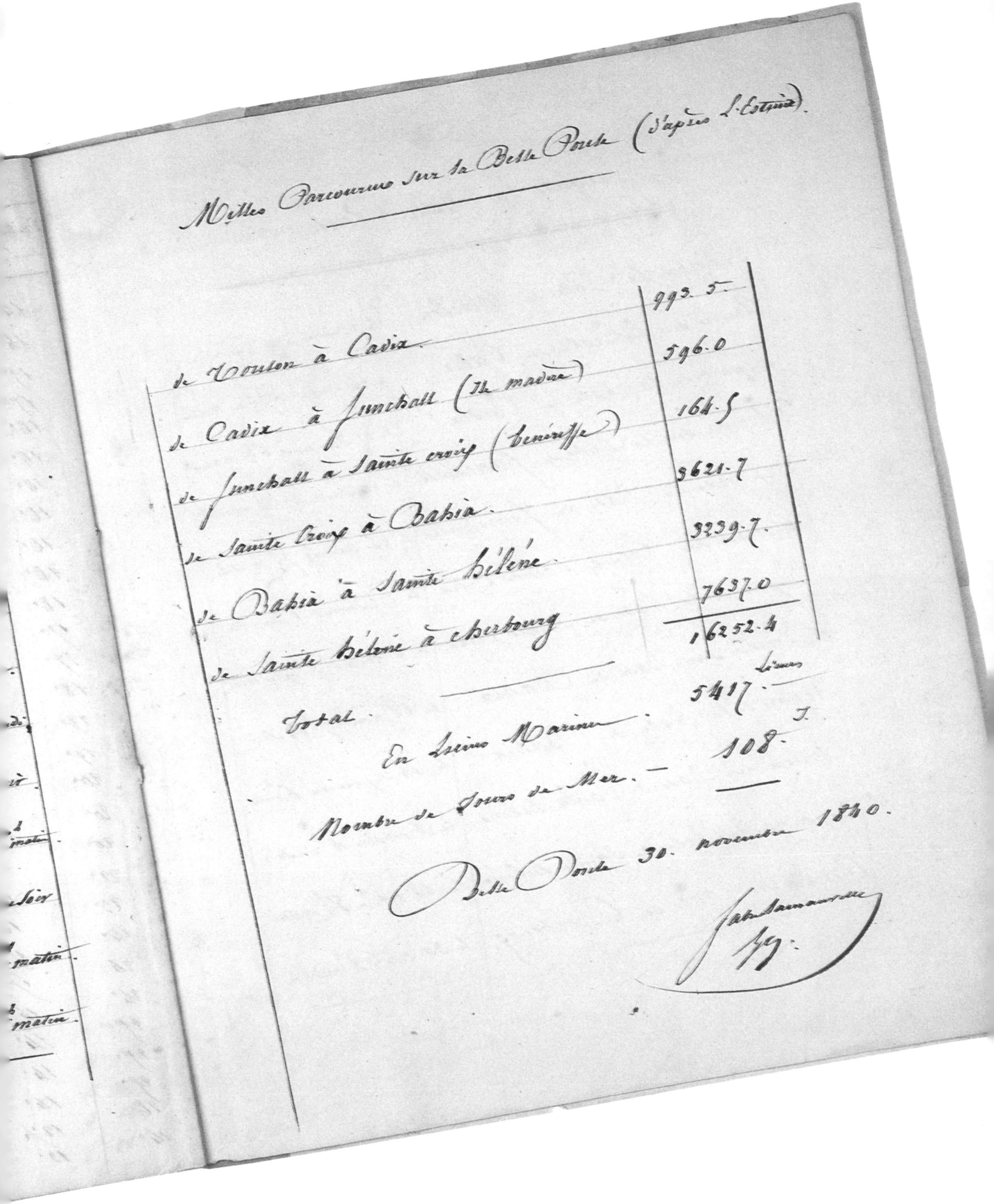

Milles Parcourus sur la Belle Poule (d'après L'Estime).

	993.5.
de Toulon à Cadix.	596.0
de Cadix à Junchall (île madère)	164.5
de Junchall à Sainte croix (ténérisse)	3621.7
de Sainte Croix à Bahia.	3239.7.
de Bahia à Sainte hélène	7637.0
de Sainte hélène à cherbourg	16252.4

total .   5417 Lieues

En Lieues Marine .   108 J.

Nombre de Jours de Mer. —

Belle Poule 30. novembre 1840.

Jat Laumardelle
4g.

MAIRIE DE SAINT-DENIS.

TRANSLATION
des Restes Mortels
DE
L'EMPEREUR NAPOLÉON.

Nous, Maire de la ville de Saint-Denis, chevalier de la Légion-d'Honneur;

Après nous être concerté avec M. le Maître des Requêtes, Sous-Préfet de l'arrondissement, et M. le Colonel de la 1re Légion;

Considérant que, par décrèt impérial du 20 Février 1806, la basilique de Saint-Denis était appelée à recevoir la sépulture de l'Empereur Napoléon, mais que des événemens au dessus des prévisions humaines ont empêché l'exécution de ce décrèt;

Considérant que les Cendres impériales, déposées depuis vingt ans dans le sein d'une terre étrangère, viennent d'être restituées à la France;

Considérant qu'en se rendant de Cherbourg à la Capitale, elles doivent passer devant le territoire de la commune, et que ne pouvant plus espérer en être les dépositaires, il nous est permis de jeter sur elles un dernier regard.

Dans le but de répondre aux vœux de nos concitoyens, en faisant une démonstration qui atteste nos sympathies et notre loyal concours aux nobles intentions du gouvernement,

Arrêtons ce qui suit :

ARTICLE PREMIER.

Le jour où la dépouille mortelle de l'Empereur passera devant notre territoire, la garde nationale de Saint-Denis prendra les armes pour escorter les autorités, et se porter sur les bords de la Seine, où des honneurs religieux et militaires seront rendus à la mémoire du grand homme.

ARTICLE 2.

Une chapelle sera élevée à l'endroit le plus convenable du rivage pour recevoir le clergé qui, interprète de nos sentimens et de nos vœux, récitera les prières des morts.

ARTICLE 3.

Le même jour, des bons de pain, viande et bois seront remis à domicile aux indigens par les soins de MM. les Membres du Bureau de Bienfaisance et des Commissaires désignés à cet effet,

Il est inutile de rappeler aux habitans de la ville, qui désireront assister à cette touchante cérémonie, que le calme et le recueillement devront être au fond de tous les cœurs, et que le moindre désordre serait un outrage à la mémoire de celui que nous voulons saluer d'un modeste mais respectueux hommage.

Saint-Denis, le 11 Décembre 1840.

Le Maire de Saint-Denis,

BRISSON.

PREVOT, imprimeur à St-Denis.

FUNÉRAILLES

DE

L'EMPEREUR.

Arrêté du Préfet.

LE PAIR DE FRANCE, CONSEILLER-D'ETAT, COMMANDEUR DE LA LÉGION D'HONNEUR, PRÉFET DE LA SEINE-INFÉRIEURE.

FROM USURPER
and ogre to the Antichrist

On 20 March 1814, just as the Eagle was landing on the towers of Notre-Dame, there appeared in Paris a pamphlet offering a witty collection of captioned images unsympathetic to the Emperor: 'The Monster has quit the Isle of Elba'; 'The Brigand has landed at the Golfe de Cannes'; 'The Usurper has entered Grenoble'; 'The Corsican has met with the authorities in Lyons'; 'Bonaparte sees his army reinforced by that of Marshal Ney'; 'The Rival of the Bourbons has revisited the room at Fontainebleau where he signed his abdication'; 'His Imperial Majesty will tonight sleep at the Tuileries.'

The war of images In their comic sequence, the tabloid-style captions cited above reflect the situation that developed during those combustible months when the black legend and the golden legend collided head-on. The dark narrative had emerged in the last months of the reign. As early as 1796, however, England's caricaturists had begun to target the 'bloody Corsican,' eventually flooding the Continent with powerfully drawn graphics utterly devastating in their irreverence, their subversive demystification of the Great Man. This counter-legend, repeated throughout Germany and Russia, also had the effect of fueling counter-revolutionary and royalist propaganda. Active between 1799 and 1804 (culminating in outrage over the execution of the Duc d'Enghien), propaganda from the opposition welled up in 1813 after the Battle of Leipzig (Napoleon's first major defeat in Germany), becoming a torrent in 1814–1815, almost full spate

even during the Hundred Days. However, it did not flow without vigorous challenge from the Napoleonic propagandists, who adopted the violet as their symbol. Alexandre Dumas explains: 'The bouquets of violets were an emblem of March, the month in which the King of Rome was born and Napoleon returned [from Elba]. Thereafter, violets became a symbol. They were worn in all kinds of ways, on the side of hats, as trimming on dresses. Some, more fanatic than others, wore a gold violet on the lapel, like an order of chivalry' (*Mes Mémoires*).

This was the heyday of England's Thomas Rowlandson and James Gillray, whose rollicking caricatures few could resist. Along with them came the Germans' send-up of the 'little man' and the 'little emperor,' forever ridiculed by the 'big general' Blücher, and the Russian bear chasing the

Caricature reacted to official iconography by offering a range of counter-representations designed to undermine the image of the Great Man.

opposite, below: W. Heath, *Boney and His Old Student, or the Devil and the Emperor on the Isle of Elba.*

opposite, above: Anonymous, *The Nonpareil General.* This French version of an original caricature by the German engraver Johann Michael Voltz appeared during the campaign in Germany. The various parts of the subject are labeled with the names of his conquests and crimes.

above: Anonymous, *The Eagle's Flight.* Prefects and mayors stand in awe as Napoleon, in March 1815, flies across southern France towards the towers of Notre-Dame.

Napoleonic fox. These graphic lampoons outdid one
another in their subversiveness, their antic scorn,
vilification, and cynicism, their ingenious terato-
logical use of the tiger, the dog, the snake, the ogre
to evoke a creature of unparalleled monstrousness.
And while the caricaturists bestialized and
demonized the Emperor, the pampleteers painted the
hideous portrait of a bloodthirsty tyrant, a
degenerate usurper, a reincarnation of Nero,
Tiberius, Attila the Hun, Gengis Khan, and
Tamerlane all rolled into one. Graphics and texts
alike were the propaganda tools thought necessary to
counter the new Alexander, the new Caesar, the new
Charlemagne! The slanders proliferated in the years
1814–1821, ceaseless in their denunciations of the
Corsican brigand, the ogre devouring France and
Europe, the exterminating demon, the scabrous,
libidinous madman, the terrifying rebirth of all the
fiendish despots, etc., etc. The alarm spread, along
with it the word that Napoleon was an all-
consuming, even sadistic villain, a savage, foreign
despot, an adventurer without faith or law. Thus did
Napoleon appear in what was an abundant literature,
a literature often enriched by the best writers,
including Chateaubriand with his *De Buonaparte et des
Bourbons* (1814).

One might imagine that come the Restoration the
black legend would truly surge. Beginning in 1817,

Most of the derision and invective aimed at Napoleon origi-
nated in England and Germany.

top: J.F.-A. Clar, *The Coronation of Napoleon I*. 1805.
This image, printed in Leipzig, mocks the *sacre* of 1804.

above: Johann Gottfried Shadow, *Concert in Leipzig*.
Here the gleeful reference is to the first major loss suffered
by the Grand Army in Germany (16–19 October 1813).

opposite: Anonymous, *Saint Napoleon, Patron of Warriors*,
1852, lithograph. This shocking image, representing the
Emperor decked out in a preposterous costume, seems to
have come in response to the anti-Bonaparte outrage triggered by Louis Napoleon's coup d'état of 2 December 1852,
which would usher in the Second Empire.

however, it began to wane, as if from a sudden loss of power, as if from its own inadequacy, from the absence of genuine popular support. In fact, the negative image remained an affair of politics and intellectuals, and it could not erase memories of the loss and the occupation. Needless to say, everyone was weary of war and hungry for rest. But the blunders of the Restoration, the arrogance of the ultra-conservatives, the haughtiness and hatred of the émigrés, who had learned nothing and forgotten nothing, the mean-spirited stupidity of those who had attempted to destroy the Vendôme Column, saved only by Allied intervention, the nauseating spectacle of the onetime adulators of the Emperor libeling him with the basest calumnies, the better to win favors from the new regime, using terms like 'despot' and 'monster' to characterize a person they had once fawned upon and called the executor of divine decrees, or yet those who brought out purported confessions of a Napoleon admitting to the worst crimes—all of this worked against the black legend and to the benefit of the fabulous prisoner. Romanticism then took over and assured the triumph of the golden legend. The Napoleon of Hugo, Dumas, and Balzac took revenge upon his enemies and Waterloo itself.

Under the July Monarchy (1830–1848)—when Louis-Philippe d'Orléans reigned as King of the French, but not King of France—the *Mémorial*, the Romantics' celebrations, and popular memory joined forces to bring back the image of the Great Man and the god of History. By the time of the July Revolution of 1830, hailed as a burst of sunlight by the historian Jules Michelet, the dark shadow of the black legend had all but disappeared. After obscuring the Napoleonic star in 1814–1815, it now vanished altogether. Never dead, however, the evil Napoleon would revive under the Second Empire.

The uncle's shadow For the rest of the century, attitudes towards Napoleon divided along lines drawn, on one side, by the republicanism, French-style, that returned to France after Napoleon III's defeat at Sedan (4 December 1870), which provided an opportunity for the Commune to bring down the Vendôme Column, and, on the other side, by the horrified memories still haunting several European countries, foremost among them Tolstoy's Russia. Needless to say, the enemies of Napoleon III attacked him through his uncle. The Second Empire damaged the myth. Napoleon suffered because of 'Naboleon,' a punning conflation of Napoleon and *nabot* meaning dwarf.

In this context, the literary scene, as always, was dominated by Victor Hugo, who, from his exile on first Jersey and then Guernsey, excoriated Napoleon the Lessor and reconsidered Napoleon the Great. *Les Châtiments* (*The Chastisements*) appeared in 1853. Here everything began with Brumaire, a crime that made

opposite: Victor Hugo, *Les Châtiments*, 1853. In this collection of poems (*The Chastisements*) Hugo appeared to use verse as a weapon with which to slay a vulture—the degraded eagle. But how could the effect have been any more devastating than that of the caricatures?

top: Anonymous, *Napoleon on Stilts.* Here the caricaturist has Napoleon doing a split while struggling to balance on stilts planted in Moscow and Madrid.

above: Anonymous, *His Name Will Appear, in Races of the Future, Even to the Cruelest Tyrants like a Means to Injure*, 1815. In this engraving Napoleon is more freighted with tyranny than Robespierre himself. The title comes from Agrippina's tirade against Nero in Racine's play *Britannicus* (1669). Such were the razor shafts that pierced the Great Man.

the future seem to unfold as if in redemption—the attainment of ultimate goals, the apotheosis of liberty—doing so in the shade of the 'holy tree of Progress.' History, poetry, and myth—all came together to create an epic of humanity triggered by an event that shaped the century. In *Les Misérables* (1862) Hugo made Napoleon an actor in a great march of progress, a progress willed by God, who then brought him down once he was no longer needed. Adolphe Thiers, in his *Histoire du Consulat et de l'Empire* (1840–1855), glorified the Napoleonism of his readers during the July Monarchy. On the other hand, the historian Jules Michelet deplored the liquidator of the Revolution, while Pierre Larousse allowed his dictionary to acknowledge a Bonaparte but not a Napoleon: 'General of the French Republic, born in Ajaccio (Isle of Corsica) on 15 August 1769, died at the Château de Saint-Cloud, near Paris, on 18 Brumaire Year VIII of the French Republic, one and indivisible.'

Left or right, historiography was practiced mainly in opposition, its dominant theme formulated by the poet/statesman Alphonse de Lamartine: 'This man, one of God's immense creations, took the path of the revolution and the improvement in the human spirit as if to stop the ideas and reverse the road to truth. One admires him as a soldier, one takes his measure as a sovereign, and one judges him as a founder of nations. Large in action, small in ideas, and a nullity in virtue. That is the man.'

In addition to history there was the novel. For an Edmond About, wittily taking on the golden legend in *The Man with the Broken Ear* (1862), the novel remained above all the domain of the writing duo Erckmann-Chatrian, in whose works the black legend was bound up with the miseries of war and the hard life of the people. Their fiction illustrated the idea that the Empire had betrayed the hopes of the Republic.

Meanwhile, another discourse came into play. An argument like none other, it was to spawn a vast progeny. In 1852 Karl Marx published *The Eighteenth Brumaire of Louis Napoleon*, which, for a long time to come, would serve as the Marxist vulgate on the subject of Napoleon III. The book provided as well an interpretation of Napoleon I, which the 20th century would take up and develop further. In the cold glare of dialectical reason, what the Great Man appeared to be was not merely a parvenu decked out, like the Revolution, in the garb of antiquity and overloaded with myths, but also an agent of progress, an objective servant of the bourgeoisie, and a

liberator of capitalist energy. 'Within France itself Napoleon . . . created the conditions whereby for the first time free competition could be developed, a property system based upon small holdings could be made profitable, and the industrial productivity of the nation, set free, could be put to use, while everywhere outside France he swept away feudal institutions, as far as was necessary to create for French bourgeois society a correspondingly up-to-date environment on the European continent. Once the new model of society had been established, the antediluvian giants disappeared, and with them a resurrected Rome—all the Brutuses, the Gracchi, the Publicolas, the tribunes and the senators, and Caesar himself.'

The dark Napoleon after 1850 Jules Michelet, in his history of the 19th century (1872–1875), drew up a veritable indictment of Napoleon I, based upon a psycho-biographical analysis of what he called the 'skillful prestidigitator.' It was his version of the black legend. Bonaparte, 'fortune's darling,' fascinated and even obsessed Michelet, who saw Napoleon as the main character in a drama that

turned the 19th century into myth rather than history. Vehemently denouncing him, the historian accused the Emperor of having distorted the very principle of history. Thus, in his own way, Michelet too subverted the efficacy of the Napoleonic myth. Hippolyte Taine went even further. In *Les Origines de la France contemporaine* (published in 1890–1893, together with sections on the Empire that had begun to appear in 1887), this positivist historian made a profoundly negative assessment of the French Revolution, whose heir he considered Bonaparte to be. For Taine, Napoleon was an uncompromising centralizer, certainly a genius, but consumed by ambition like none other, a young Italian who despised France. Here the black legend reappeared in a new combinational analysis, one involving an historical person far beyond the ordinary, a figure not reducible to any norm or category. More than a foreigner, he was totally different: 'Manifestly, he is neither a Frenchman nor a man of the 18th century; he belongs to another race and to another age.'

While the republican opposition denounced Napoleon as a way of getting at the Second Empire, the black legend took on even darker colors abroad, especially in Russia. In 1880 Tchaikovsky completed his *1812 Overture*, a symphonic re-enactment of the epic Russian campaign. Already in 1868, Tolstoy had made Napoleon a player in *War and Peace*, a variable figure whose look and character change as the story unfolds. The dominant image, however, is that of the Antichrist, simultaneously the hydra of the Revolution and a monster dedicated to evil in all its forms. Imbued with superhuman pride, by turns wily, insensitive, or even affable, he acquires a powerfully dramatic dimension by the time of Borodino (7 September 1812). Solitary in the Romantic tradition, isolated in his excessiveness, Tolstoy's Napoleon ends up merely a cynic whose egoism leaves him indifferent to men's death.

Reproduced on these facing pages are two portraits of the same family, Republican in 1849 and Imperial after 1852. In the latter the King of Rome—Duke of Reichstadt to his Hapsburg relatives and Napoleon II to Bonapartists—stands to the right of his father, while Napoleon III stands to the left. In the foreground the Prince Imperial (Louis Napoleon), the only child of Napoleon III and Empress Eugénie, who would perish in Africa while serving with the British.

above: Calendar, 1849.

opposite: Jules Didier, *Four Generations of Bonapartes*, after 1852.

ENE MENE,
TEKEL,
JPHARSIN

above: James Gillray, *The Handwriting on the Wall*, published on 24 April 1803. One of Englan's most effective caricaturists, Gillray quoted Michelangelo's famous representation of a scene from Genesis by way of alluding to the Cadoudal conspiracy. Three days before the appearance of this graphic, Georges Cadoudal had left London for Paris with the intention of assassinating Bonaparte, a fact known to Gillray.

opposite: Johann Michael Voltz, *Triumph of the Year 1813*. This satiric engraving, one of the most famous ever made in Germany, sold some 20,000 copies in Berlin and found a ready market throughout Europe. Note, once again, the hand of God, this time as an epaulette. The bust, shaped like the map of Germany, bears the names of the year's battles, among them Leipzig, Napoleon's first important loss. The face is composed of cadavers and the hat of the Prussian eagle, not the eagle of Imperial France. For the English version seen here, a text has been added listing Napoleon's titles and deeds, all of them parodied.

NAPOLEON

THE FIRST, and LAST, by the Wrath of Heaven Emperor of the Jacobins, Protector of the Confederation of Rogues, Mediator of the Hellish League, Grand Cross of the Legion of Horror, Commander in Chief of the Legions of Skeletons left at Moscow, Smolensk, Leipzig, &c. Head Runner of Runaways, Mock High-Priest of the Sanhedrim, Mock Prophet of Mussulmen, Mock Pillar of the Christian Faith, Inventor of the Syrian Method of disposing of his own Sick by sleeping Draughts, or of captured Enemies by the Bayonet; First Grave-Digger for burying alive; Chief Gaoler of the Holy Father and of the King of Spain, Destroyer of Crowns, and Manufacturer of Counts, Dukes, Princes, and Kings; Chief Douanier of the Continental System, Head Butcher of the Parisian and Toulonese Massacres, Murderer of Hoffer, Palm, Wright, nay, of his own Prince, the noble and virtuous Duke of Enghien, and of a thousand others; Kidnapper of Ambassadors, High-Admiral of the Invasion Praams, Cup-Bearer of the Jaffa Poison, Arch-Chancellor of Waste-Paper Treaties, Arch-Treasurer of the Plunder of the World, the sanguinary Coxcomb, Assassin, and Incendiary......to

MAKE PEACE WITH!!!

Napoleon: The Immortal Emperor

COPY

OF THE

𝕿𝖗𝖆𝖓𝖘𝖕𝖆𝖗𝖊𝖓𝖈𝖞

EXHIBITED AT

ACKERMANN'S REPOSITORY OF ARTS,

During the Illuminations of the 5th and 6th of November, 1813,

IN HONOUR OF THE SPLENDID VICTORIES OBTAINED BY

The ALLIES over the ARMIES of FRANCE,

AT LEIPSIC AND ITS ENVIRONS.

───────────

THE TWO KINGS OF TERROR.

This Subject, representing the two Tyrants, viz. the Tyrant Bonaparte and the Tyrant Death, sitting together on the Field of Battle, in a manner which promises a more perfect intimacy immediately to ensue, is very entertaining. It is also very instructing to observe, that the former is now placed in a situation in which all Europe *may see through him.* The emblem, too, of the Circle of dazzling light from mere *vapour*, which is so *soon extinguished*, has a good moral effect; and as the Gas represents the dying flame, so does the Drum, on which he is seated, typify the *hollow* and *noisy* nature of the falling Usurper.

The above description of the subject appeared in the *Sun* of Saturday, the 6th of November. These pointed comments arose from the picture being *transparent*, and from a Circle, indicative of the strength and brotherly union of the Allies, which surmounted the same, composed of *gas* of brilliant brightness.

opposite, above: James Gillray, *The King of Brobdingnag*, 1804. While George III plays himself, Napoleon becomes tiny Gulliver attempting to maneuver his toy sailboat in a box-like reservoir—i.e., invade England in 1803–1804. By adopting characters from the satires of Jonathan Swift, Gillray hit upon a rich thematic lode—the dwarf Bonaparte or Napoleon—which would also be mined by the pamphleteers.

opposite, below: James Gillray. *Tiddy Doll the Great French Gingerbread Maker, Drawing out a New Batch of Kings; His Man, Talley, Mixing up the Dough*, 1806. A clear reference to Napoleon's latest creation: the Confederation of the Rhine.

left: Thomas Rowlandson, *Death and Bonaparte or the Two Kings of Terror*, c. 1813, colored etching. As this graphic implies, Napoleon met his match at the Battle of Leipzig, the first major defeat suffered by the Grand Army. The image replicates a transparent painting exhibited at the Ackermann art shop in London during the illuminations staged on 5 and 6 November 1813.

below: Anonymous, *The Great Extinguisher*, 1813. A motif frequently used by the caricaturists, the extinguisher, or candle-snuffer, is in this instance played by a Cossack.

above: Anonymous, *Departure for the Army*, colored etching copyrighted 12 June 1815. Here the date is significant, anticipating as it did the Waterloo disaster that would come six days later. Note not only the skeletal horse but also the eagle with its tongue hanging out.

right: Frédéric Dubois, *Napoleon Invades England, Finally*, August 1815, colored etching. Again the date is important, since it coincides generally with the presence of Napoleon on board the HMS *Bellerophon* anchored off Ply-

mouth, a prisoner of the English prior to his deportation to St. Helena on 9 August. A Wellington-like British officer escorts the Emperor, downcast and in chains, from one boat to another, the HMS *Northumberland*, for the long voyage to St. Helena.

opposite: Anonymous, *The New Robinson Crusoe on St. Helena*, 1816. Here the caricaturist, though nameless, was French, acknowledging an English victory. Note the eagle serving as a finial on the fallen umbrella.

FROM NATIONAL HERO
to the victor of 1918

L'Empereur

In 1871 the Commune that seized Paris and other French cities, following the French defeat in the brief Franco-Prussian War, knocked down the Vendôme Column, symbolically liquidating Bonapartism. The great bronze pile would be restored in 1874, at the expense of the painter Gustave Courbet, a ringleader in what had been an 'official' act of vandalism. Meanwhile, the decree of 12 April 1871, authorizing the destruction, summarized the anti-Bonapartist argument: 'The Commune of Paris, considering that the Imperial column in the Place Vendôme is a monument to barbarism, a symbol of brute force and false glory, an affirmation of militarism, a negation of international law, a permanent insult by the victors to the vanquished, a perpetual attack upon one of the three great principles of the French Republic, Fraternity. Decreed: Sole article. —The column in the Place Vendôme shall be demolished.'

This decision would not be ratified by the Third Republic (1871–1940). Still, tensions raged over the Napoleonic legacy, reflected nowhere more than in the works of Louis-Ernest Meissonier and Édouard Detaille. Born in 1815, the year of Waterloo, Meissonier had, in 1861, portrayed Napoleon III at the Battle of Solferino, a French victory, six years before he completed his masterpiece, *The French Campaign, 1814*. Here, against a background of snow-covered fields and a leaden sky, the Emperor, followed by his pensive aide-de-camp, sits astride a white horse, leading the troops

above and opposite: Louis-Ernest Meissonier, *Napoleon on Horseback.* Albeit sketches, these two works clearly reveal the talent of a painter who figured among the most important artists committed to the Napoleonic epic, a story Meissonier planned to illustrate in a cycle of five canvases. He had particular success with two battles scenes, Jena and Friedland. In his career, Meissonier achieved immense distinction, becoming one of the best-paid artists of the century.

while lost in thought, his jaw set and his face expressionless. The painting, albeit characteristically small in actual size, captures the immensity of the fall that was about to happen. It marks the apogee of a genre in which Eugène Isabey also excelled, as already seen in *Lowering the Coffin onto the Belle-Poule, 15 October 1840* (pages 144–145). Ingres too made a significant contribution with his *Apotheosis of Napoleon I* (study, page 128), painted for a ceiling in Paris's Hôtel de Ville but then destroyed by fire in 1871. Édouard Detaille, a pupil of Meissonier who specialized in military subjects, revived the Napoleonic legend in *The Dream*, a work of 1888. The very size of this painting—3 meters by 4—seems to register the epic wind sweeping through *Le Rêve passe*, a 1906 song it evidently inspired. 'The Dream Passes,' with lyrics by Foucher and music by Helmer and Krier, exemplifies the songs of revenge, a revenge the Third Republic was preparing with the help of the man in the mouse-colored greatcoat: 'The soldiers are over there asleep on the plain / . . . In the sky all of a sudden cavalry without number / Strike thunderbolts and brighten the vague clarity / And the Little Hat appears, leading the shades / Towards immortality.'

The professor of energy Out of the defeat and fall of Napoleon III, on 4 September 1870, rose the Third French Republic, a government that might have been expected to reject the great ancestor. On the contrary, the Republic would

simply annex him. After all, revenge had to be exacted and Alsace/Lorraine recovered. Who, better than the hero of Jena, could recharge the national batteries? Napoleon with his eye fixed on that blue line in the Vosges. Popular fiction spread the Napoleonic legend, thanks to the cheap collections and huge printings issued by Fayard, Ollendorff, and Tallander. The novelist Georges d'Esparbès glorified the Eagle and his veterans, while the Provençal writer Mistral beat the drum for the little hero of Arcola. Along with the novels came the *Mémoires* of soldiers (Coignet, Marbot, Parquin, Thiébault), a deluge of pictorial works (paintings by Boutigny, Charlier, Detaille, and Marchand, not to mention all the postal cards), and a veritable orgy of songs, patriotic ('Le Régiment de Sambre et Meuse' [1870], 'Le Père la Victoire' [1888]), bellicose ('Le Clairon' [1875]), or amusingly militaristic ('Le 113e de ligne' [1881]). The existence of a Bonapartist press, such as *Le Petit Caporal* (1876–1914), also carried the word: Napoleon was a national hero. He had only to become a Republican hero. To this end, popular novels contributed enormously, with their rich stews of Romanticism and republican ideology, wild adventure and sentimental plots, vivid characters and heroic values.

In 1884 Ernest Lavisse—the quasi-official historian of the Third Republic (the 'national school-teacher,' as Pierre Nora called him)—offered a textbook version of Napoleon, condemned as a despot but also admired as the victorious Emperor. The First Empire became a glorious point of reference for the schoolchildren of Republican France. A dark picture festooned in the three colors of the Grand Army. Thus Napoleon became a warrior model for younger generations, joining Charlemagne, Joan of Arc, and Henri IV to complete the central quartet within the curriculum of national history taught in French schools. The Republic needed him in order to shore up its legitimacy. School syllabi went hand in glove with literature aimed at young people, such as Montorgueil's *Bonaparte* illustrated by Job (1910, followed in 1921 by the same author's *Napoléon*) and Ernest Lajeunesse's *L'Imitation de notre maître Napoléon* (1896). The generation that would be slaughtered in 1914 was thoroughly indoctrinated in the cult of the Consular and Imperial years. As Jean Tulard so delightfully put it, the Empire looked beautiful under the Republic. Of course, the successor to Jena would be Verdun. The Republic

recruited Napoleon Bonaparte and made him don the sky-blue uniform. The tomb in the Invalides led to the trenches of 1914–1918. It was on the eve of these horrors that Napoleon, the professor of energy, made his entrance. The novelist Maurice Barrès, in *Les Déracinés* (1897), attempted to reveal the true Napoleon buried under all the other Napoleons constructed by history, a Napoleon with the features of Bonaparte: 'Here then is what does not die, that person who sustained the Emperor in all his realities, and who supports his legend at every stage of his immortality. And so just as his sharp medallion profile, more than the many stigmatas he suffered and the many aspects of genius he displayed, became the definitive and proper stand-in for his body once life had ended the cycle of his activity, it is necessary that, after all the transformations in the legend, one arrive at this: NAPOLEON, PROFESSOR OF ENERGY.'

The new apotheosis André Suarès, in his *Napoléon* (*Cahiers de la Quinzaine*, 1912; revised and expanded in 1933 under the title *Vues sur Napoléon*), evoked the man of the Revolution, the man of destiny, the 'sovereign spectacle of action.' Like Joan of Arc, he was 'a supreme moment in the human race.' Moreover, 'France never ceases to be vain about it, like a woman whose husband was the master of all men. She cannot think of him without trembling and in her trembling, however much she may miss him, she also fears him; she fears what she still misses.' Napoleon or the soul of France? Both the theatre and Léon Bloy would answer the question, each in its/his own manner.

With Edmond Rostand's *L'Aiglon* (1900) Napoleon made his grand return to the stage, following *Madame Sans-Gêne*, a play by Victorien Sardou and Émile Moreau, which had its premiere at the Théâtre du Vaudeville on 27 October 1893. In the latter, 'History found itself reworked by fantasy. Rostand, on the other hand, wrote an historical drama in high, Romantic style, a play, with a cross-dressed Sarah Bernhardt in the title role, that was to become one of the attractions of the great Universal Exposition in 1900. Here the Napoleonic myth merged with the tragic destiny of a young man—the only child of Napoleon and Marie-Louise—crushed under the weight of History. The elegiac and doleful theme unfolded in stark contrast to the heroic mood so eloquently conveyed by the character Flambeau, a veteran of the Emperor's Old Guard.

Léon Bloy made his 1912 novel *L'Âme de Napoléon* (*The Soul of Napoleon*) an unabashed profession of faith, an act of worship that celebrated 'the most glorious of all mortels.' In the course of the narrative he also developed an explicit messianic conception, thereby merging the continuity of mystical Romanticism, close in spirit to the visions of Gérard de Nerval, whose posthumous sonnet 'The Armed Head' ('La Tête armée') associated l'Aiglon with Christ: 'The one spilled his blood to fertilize the earth, / The other sowed Heaven with the seed of the Gods!' Bloy's Napoleon, more supernatural than superhuman, subsumed all the legendary, mythic images and became a 'poet of destiny.'

Later, only the cinema, apart from the art historian Élie Faure, would succeed in recapturing such ringing tones of conviction. For the

above: Louis-Ernest Meissonier, *The French Campaign, 1814*, 1867. Here, in one of the artist's masterpieces, the weary attitude of the generals—Drouot, Berthier, and Flahut—is in marked contrast to the fierce, somber determination written across the face of the Emperor. This canvas, along with the portrait by Delaroche, who portrayed Napoleon after the fall (page 134), is unquestionably one of the definitive images of the hero in his decline—the titan who would tumble but who still marches, albeit surrounded by the shattered remains of his power. Even in defeat, he evinces the energy celebrated by Barrès.

Republican nation itself, there remained but one last chance to consecrate the Great Man, this time by associating him with the victory of 1918. Marking the centenary of the Emperor's death, Marshal Foch delivered an eloquent tribute at the porphyry tomb in the Invalides: 'Sire, sleep in peace. From the tomb itself you still labor for France. Always in times of threat to the nation, our flags flutter as the Eagle takes flight. If our legions have returned victorious by way of the triumphal

next. If public sentiment fell short of consensus, the Emperor nonetheless rallied the core of the nation, at least for a time.

Yet even Foch's laudatory address pales in comparison with the book written by Élie Faure, whose Napoleon remains the most beautiful illustration ever written of the heroic superman of our century. With Faure, the Romantic conception of Napoleon attained its apogee. Napoleon the poet of action, Prometheus Napoleon, Napoleon the

arch which you built, it is because that Austerlitz sword had indicated the direction by showing us how to unite and lead the forces that brought victory. Your brilliant lessons, your relentless endeavor remain everlasting examples. As we study and reflect upon them, the art of war grows larger with every passing day. It is only by the radiance reverently and carefully gathered from your immortal glory that future generations will, for a long time to come, understand the science of combat and the maneuver of armies, for the sacred cause of defending the country.' Thus appropriated by the victor of 1918, Napoleon, more than ever, played the national hero, increasingly absorbed into the Republican continuity from one century to the

most decisive actor on the human stage since Jesus Christ—all presented with singular power at a time when new revolutionary messianisms were on the rise. Faure, without doubt, realized the best synthesis of the mythic aspects of the great man, that artist of history who opened the human will to perspectives never before imagined. Everything about him called forth superlatives. Model of human freedom, dedicated to inherent, inner solitude of the highest degree, Napoleon counts among the rare figures in modern history comparable to the great men of antiquity. Poet and artist, he shines as a creator of myths: 'He stands apart like Jesus. Çakya-Mouni [Buddha] is far from us, lost in the musky fog of Asia's marshes.

Mohammed is no more than a law-giver, like Moses or Solon. Michelangelo, Shakespeare, Rembrandt, Beethoven work outside the plan of action. They dream it, whereas Christ and Napoleon act out their dream instead of dreaming their action. Between these two summits, everyone hesitates. All about is but a fog of uncertainty, scruples, indecision, mediocrity. Nothing but a quicksand of words. Among all men, these two dared. Even unto martyrdom. Unto death. As for moral excuses, I am

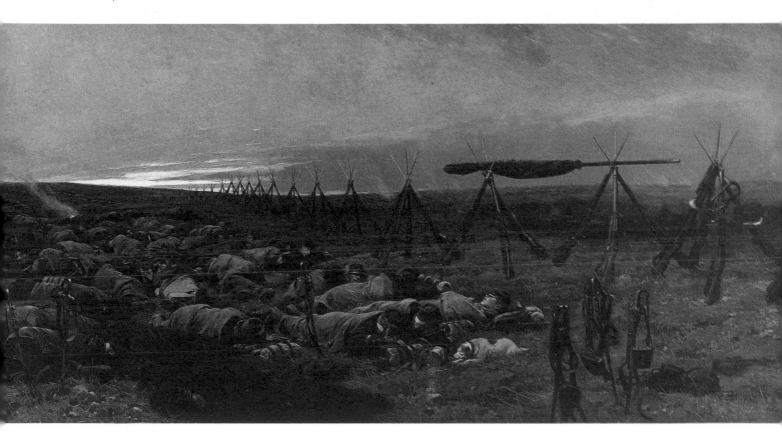

not eager to acknowledge them. Moral excuses are masks placed by men on the impassable face of God. An instinct for domination as irresistible as the movement of the planets has maintained these two lone beings in the closed and fixed orbit of an implacable destiny. They explored to the outer limits of their nature, a nature so generous in its original power that it drove each of them to invade everything about them, to consume everything with their fire, including the crowds that followed them, even themselves, moving towards an invisible goal that neither could see. They are two lone shades, known here below by Prometheus.' The Mass has been said; it remains only to be placed on stage. This would be the task of Abel Gance.

opposite: Édouard Detaille, *The Evening of Jena*, 1890. With the painting reproduced here, Detaille, a specialist in military scenes, completed a cycle of pictures dedicated to this crushing victory over Prussia. The series had been inaugurated by Charles Thévenin and then continued by Horace Vernet and Meissonier.

above: Édouard Detaille, *The Dream*, 1888. Here the artist became even more clearly identified with the theme of revenge.

Napoleon is inexplicable and, without doubt, the most inexplicable of men, because he is, beyond all else, the prefiguration of Him who must come and who may not be too far distant, a prefiguration and a precursor quite near to us, himself identified by all the extraordinary men who preceded him in the whole of time . . . . What therefore did he come to do in that 18th-century France, which of course did not foresee him and expected him even less? None other than this: a gesture from God through the French so that people all over the world might not forget that there truly is a God and that He will come like a thief in the night, at an hour no one knows, with such utter astonishment that it will bring about the exinanition of the Universe.

It was no doubt necessary that this gesture be undertaken by a man who scarcely believed in God and who knew nothing of the Commandments. Since he had never been invested as either a Patriarch or a Prophet, it was important that he be unaware of his Mission, any more than a storm or an earthquake would be, so that he could be likened by his enemies to an Antichrist or a demon. Most of all, it was essential that the Revolution—the irreparable ruin of the Old World—be consummated by him. Evidently God wanted nothing more to do with that old world. He wanted new things, and a Napoleon was needed to bring them on. The exodus, which took the lives of millions of men . . . .

Nothing about Napoleon can be understood as long as he is not viewed as a poet, an incomparable poet in action. His poem is his entire life, and there is nothing else like it. Always he thought as a poet and could act only as he thought, the visible world being for him nothing but a mirage.

Léon Bloy, *L'Âme de Napoléon* (1912)

The stricken features of the fallen giant, marked with the memory of his past glory, are particularly well captured in these two portraits.

above: James Sant, *The Last Phase*, 1901. Commissioned by Lord Rosebery, this portrait is remarkable for its realism.

opposite: Xavier-Alphonse Monchablon, *Napoleon Late in Life*. Here the exiled Emperor looks truly haunted.

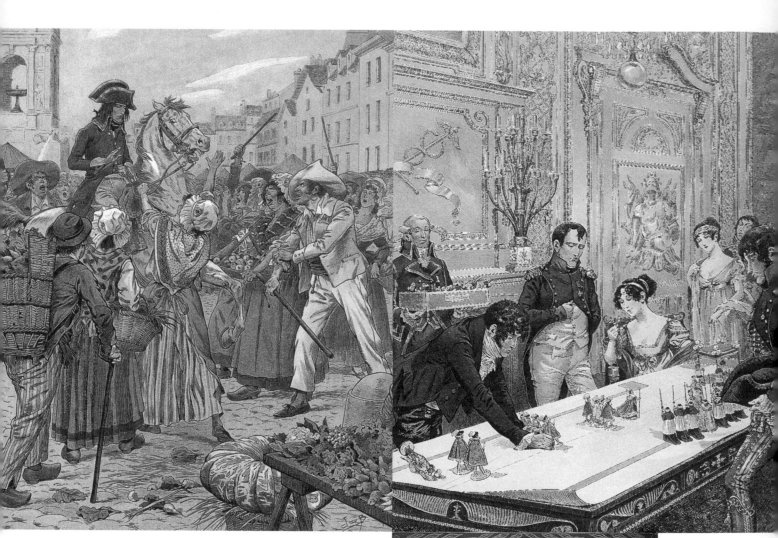

Job (Jacques Onfroy de Bréville;1858–1931) was one of France's foremost designers and illustrators at the end of the 19th century and the beginning of the 20th. A caricaturist, Job also specialized in the illustration of children's literature, most particularly works dealing with history. His big illustrated volumes were frequently given as prizes. Under the Third Republic, grammar schools, given the task of fostering a sense of national unity, built a curriculum steeped in patriotic values. The three images seen on these two pages are watercolors executed for reproduction in *Bonaparte de Montorgueil* (1910):

above, left: A conversation between Bonaparte and a merchant in Les Halles. the vast central food market in Paris.

above, right: Rehearsal for the coronation, directed by Jean-Baptiste Isabey using dolls of his own creation.

opposite: A picnic in the gardens at Malmaison, hosted by the First Consul and Josephine.

right: The cover of the book.

opposite: Réjane (Gabrielle-Charlotte Réju; 1856–1920), one of modern France's greatest actresses, in the title role of *Madame Sans-Gêne* (1893) by Victorien Sardou, famous for his 'well-made plays.'

right and below: Sarah Bernhardt (1844–1923), an equally great and even more famous actress, created the title role in *L'Aiglon*, by the Romantic playwright Edmond Rostand, on 15 March 1900 and in the theatre named for her. An unprecedented success, the play ran for 250 performances during the year of the Universal Exposition. The *comédienne*, a genuine legend in her own right, was very much in tune with the Napoleonic myth. Meticulous about costume, Bernhardt chose for the second act the uniform of the Royal Hungarian Regiment—white wool with green facing—in which the Duke of Reichstadt was most often represented. '

NAPOLEON
a myth of the 20th century

The Napoleons

of the 20th century...

From the 19th century until today, the narrative has continued along the same course. That is, everybody invents his own Napoleon, consistent with preferred ideologies and aesthetics. He remains one of the truly salient figures of the modern era, a period rich in charismatic leaders, and he is present in the great conflicts that still rend the world. Dreams, symbols, recuperations, identifications, demonizations—in all these forms and more do modern politics appropriate the Emperor, serving him up to suit every cause, including totalitarianism. Positions for and against may still be taken, but the processes of heroicization and mythification go on, benefiting from new forms of expression. Indeed, they found a truly remarkable exponent in Abel Gance, *auteur* of a grandiose and visionary film. The cinema, for all its power to dominate, cannot stifle Napoleonic imagery. Long after the likes of Gros, the Vernets, and Meissonier, Surrealist painters treated the Napoleonic theme in their own fashion, among them Magritte in *The Future of Statues* (1937), with its variations on the Emperor's death mask, Max Ernst in his *Napoleon in the Desert* (1941), and Ulrich Bernhardt in *Napoleon and Georg Kerner*. And let us not forget what is a vigorous academic tradition, carried on by such artists as Chapelain-Midy, Édouard Mac'Avoy, and Georges Rohner. Increasingly in the forefront, however, are the historians, who, while sharpening the analysis of the Consular and Imperial years, take a critical interest in the makeup of the myth as well as the legend, its modalities and avatars. As for writers, they include, without impairing, Napoleon in the pantheon of literary subjects and work him through every variation, in every key and on every note, from declamation to parody, from fantasy to science fiction. Indeed, the Little Hat still stands tall on the cultural horizon of the 20th century and its aftermath.

Portrayed on posters, chromos, and even banknotes, Napoleon continued to be an imposing, universal icon even in the 20th century.

opposite: Poster entitled *Napoleon Reviewing His Past*, created for the centenary of the Empire celebrated in 1904.

right: Larry Rivers, *French Money*, private collection, 1962. For his portrait of Napoleon, the American Pop artist found a model in a 100-franc note.

NAPOLEON
superstar

From Gancian epic to modern kitsch, Napoleon has appeared in every conceivable form of spectacle and multimedia. Such price glory? Very much a presence in the glittering world of theatrical make-believe, the Emperor also occupies a more than honorable place on the field of contemporary literature. The human imagination always seems prepared to give him a warm welcome.

From stage to screen The cinema reinvented Napoleon, or, put another way, it universalized his myth through the magic of moving images. The process began as early as the turn of the 19th century, or even in 1798, with the coming of the phantasmagorias, panoramas, and other types of diorama projected by magic lanterns, shadow shows, optical vues, and anamorphoses. In 1838 Frédéric Soulié, an important writer in the Romantic period, today unjustly neglected, took up the theme in *Magic Lantern: The History of Napoleon by Two Soldiers*. The age of photography had all but arrived and along with it positive plates for projection, rather like transparencies on glass. The shadow shows would attain their perfection at a popular Montmartre cabaret known as the Chat Noir, where in 1886 Caran d'Ache presented his *Épopée*, an 'epic' in thirty and then fifty tableaux, to great success.

In 1895 everything changed, after the Lumière brothers introduced the cinematograph, making possible the first moving pictures. This invention would provide the Emperor with an opportunity to dominate the world all over again, in more than 700 films of every sort, not to mention all those made for television. The Napoleonic movies range from the first major Pathé production entitled *The Napoleonic Epic*, issued in 1903, to *Napoléon*, a series of four films realized in 2002 by Yves Simoneau with Christian Clavier in the title role.

The cinema gobbled up the entire repertoire of 19th-century Napoleonic imagery, as if to sacrilize the historical fictions perpetrated by Napoleon himself. Finally Abel Gance arrived on the scene,

'Cinegraphic epic' was how Abel Gance characterized his *Napoléon* (1927), a film that did for the Great Man what Shakespeare's *Henry V* did for the victor of Agincourt—create a sublime vision. The director caused many new opinions to be formed, sending readers back to texts ranging from Alphonse Aulard to Frédéric Masson, from Bourrienne and Chateaubriand to Hugo. The photograph above records a scene in an auberge near Toulon in 1793. Bonaparte, having just arrived to take command of the French artillery, points to the Aiguillette fort on the map, calling it the key to the siege. On his right, the incompetent General Carteaux bursts out laughing, surrounded by officers and a delegation from the Paris Convention.

declaring: 'It is not . . . to produce an ordinary historical film that I have attempted to revive, in the language of images, the prodigious figure of someone who declared himself a bit of rock hurled into space; but because Napoleon is the world in summary. . . . He is a being whose arms are not long enough to embrace something larger than himself: the Revolution. Napoleon is a paroxysm in his own time, which is a paroxysm in Time. And for me the cinema is the paroxysm of life.' Of the six parts Gance planned for his titanic work, he would realize only one.

Released in 1927, *Napoléon vu par Abel Gance*, an extraordinary work of synthetic dramatization, adheres to both the legend and the myth as elaborated throughout the 19th century. Mutilated, reworked, and reconstituted, the film relies on a well-established historical tradition, however fanciful, and includes several imaginary sequences to boot, among them an unforgettable visit to the deserted Convention hall where the ghosts of the Revolution address Bonaparte prior to his departure for the Italian campaign. The scene brings the film to a close. Gance wrote a cinematic symphony—'music of light' as he described it—making himself the heir of Romanticism, which he not only assumed and but also magnified. Finally, this epic was animated by an actor who himself became mythic. By dent of his own character, Albert Dieudonné created a sublime Bonaparte. He even had the same stature as the historical model.

After Gance Subsequently a whole string of distinguished actors would play Napoleon Bonaparte. The French stars include Charles Vanel (Karl Grüne's *Waterloo* [1929]), Jean-Louis Barrault, Daniel Gélin, and Raymond Pellegin (the films of Sacha Guitry), Charles Boyer (Clarence Brown's *Conquest* or *Marie Walewska* [1937]), Pierre Mondy (Gance's *Austerlitz* [1960]), Daniel Mesguich (Robert Mazoyer's telefilm *Joséphine ou la Comédie des ambitions* [1979]), and Patrice Chéreau (Youssef Chahine's *Adieu Bonaparte* [1984]). Foreign actors too have found the Emperor an irresistible part to play, among them Werner Krauss and Claude Rains (Frank Borzage's *Hearts Divided* [1936]), Marlon Brando (Henry Koster's *Désirée* [1954]), and Rod Steiger (Serguei Bondartchuk's *Waterloo* [1970]). In *Austerlitz* Abel Gance demolished the mythological portrait he had painted in his great fresco-like film of 1927. This time he endowed the Emperor with a degree of

ambiguity, expressed through intentions and behavior, and thereby moved the picture closer to reality.

The other great minister of Napoleonic religion in the world of films was none other than Sacha Guitry, evident mainly in his *Napoléon*, made in 1955 with Daniel Gélin as Bonaparte and Raymond Pellegrin as Napoleon. Guitry identified the Emperor with France and revived the theme of providential destiny. Among the most significant of recent movies should be cited *Adieu Bonaparte*, directed by Youssef Chahine. Here Bonaparte confronts General Cafrelli, the pair of them becoming agents of two different conceptions and two different legacies of the Enlightenment. In its

PALAIS DES SPORTS
PORTE DE VERSAILLES

mise en scène
ROBERT HOSSEIN

écrit par
ALAIN DECAUX
de l'Académie Française

avec la participation de
PAUL LOMBARD

à partir du
1er OCT
2002

C'était
BONAPARTE

opposite and above: Numerous theatre pieces have been created with Napoleon Bonaparte as the principal subject. Both of the posters seen here show Egypt's Pyramids in the background. The English comic opera appears to have been somewhat in the spirit of the Gillray and Rowlandson caricatures made in the early 19th century. *C'était Bonaparte* (2002) was the latest major production directed by Robert Hossein.

own way, the film reflects not only contemporary debates over the relationship between the Enlightenment, the Revolution, and Napoleon Bonaparte, but also the diffusion of ideas about progress, war, and colonialism.

As for Hollywood, only twice has it seen fit to make Napoleon a principal character, in *Conquest* (or *Marie Walewska*) directed by Clarence Brown, who cast Charles Boyer as the Emperor and a passionate Greta Garbo as the Polish Countess, and in Henry Koster' *Désirée* starring Marlon Brando and Jean Simmons.

Soviet films took Napoleon more seriously. Vladimir Petrov shot *Kutusov* in 1943 after the Battle of Stalingrad and at the same sites where the Battle of Borodino had taken place. Stalinist ideology dictated that the defeated conqueror be viewed as the Hitler of 1812. The small screen, meanwhile, exploits the enduring sense of French identity and periodically offers programs, made-for-TV films, and debates dealing with Napoleonic themes.

Theatre, although earlier in its involvement with Napoleon but vastly surpassed by painting in quality of work, has produced some six hundred plays on the subject. Even in the 20th century, theatre made its contribution albeit in declining numbers. Saint-Georges de Bouhélier's *Napoléon* (1933) and Paul Raynal's *Napoléon unique* (1937) no longer speak to us. For better results we must look to the poet Paul Claudel, whose *L'Otage* (1911) takes place during the Revolution and Empire, or to Sacha Guitry and his *Histoire de France* (1929), or yet to musical reviews, such as the one by Serge Lama, a program of tableaux and songs filmed in Montreal in 1988. One play that truly stands out is Jean Anouilh's *La Foire d'empoigne (Free-for-All)*, which had its premiere in 1961. Impressive by reason of the author's manifest talent, the play is remarkable as well for one of its themes: purification. With tongue deep in cheek, Anouilh chronicles the Hundred Days, which he begins with an ironic disclaimer: 'Any resemblance to Napoleon or Louis XVIII must be understood as merely fortuitous and coincidental.' He then proceeds to pit an apolitical Louis XVIII, good-humored, tending simultaneously towards tolerance and ingratitude, against a cynical, disillusioned Napoleon, an impertinent adventurer and gifted show-off, busy orchestrating his legend even as he boards the HMS *Bellerophon*. At the premiere, Paul Merisse assumed both roles.

To illustrate the spread of Napoleonic antecedents into every conceivable domain, we have only to cite the ballets of Serge Lifar: *À la mémoire d'un héros*, choreographed to the music of Beethoven and mounted in 1946 with Ludmila Tcherina in the role of Bonaparte, and *Bonaparte à Nice*, a work of 1960. The Emperor even found his way onto ice, when, not long ago, artistic skating adopted an Imperial theme for one of its competitions, pursued in glides and spangles.

Napoleon in all literary genres Before Malraux, there had already been Joseph Delteil and his *Il était une fois Napoléon* (1929), a work that falls somewhere between biography and true story. Delteil, with his seductive and imagistic language, hued close to the right side of the myth and celebrated a figure overflowing with dreams: 'They tried to whitewash Napoleon, to make him a lover of peace, a League of Nations, the delight of young women, etc., in brief to make him "human." Huge mistake! To humanize a god is literally to diminish him. . . . Napoleon is a man who carries a dream in his heart. And, no doubt, we are all Napoleons. . . . Every dream with its Indies, because to live is to dream one's life. The only difference is that we do not believe in the dream, something contraband, a little girl's doll, whereas for Napoleon to dream and to do are one and the same. He realizes his dream straight away; he brings it to life at the crack of dawn, flesh and bone, while we, a useless key, we leave it in our pocket. . . .'

In addition there was André Suarès and his *Vues sur Napoléon* (1933): 'Him, it is not enough for him to dare; he is already and fully all that he dares. He is a master in every endeavor. He is the universe itself, and his life is a duel between Napoleon and the world.' Then came André Malraux, the bard of great men, who had the imagination to write *Vie de Napoléon par lui-même* (1930), a fictitious but meticulously documented journal kept by the Emperor himself. From it emerges the image of a hero fully in control of himself. A Nietzschean superman comes to mind, as the 'author,' in thought and word, reveals himself a grand organizer, a great strategist, a defender of the Revolution, and the unifier of modern Europe. Another important work is Louis Aragon's *La Semaine sainte* (*Holy Week* [1958]) in which the shadow of Napoleon falls over a plot involving the painter Théodore Géricault and the royalist exiles in Ghent during the Hundred Days.

Outside France as well as within, the true literary phenomenon arising from the fascination with Napoleon has been the proliferation of historical novels, novelized biographies, and similar concoctions. Here the usual specialists in these genres compete for the favor of a huge audience always avid for Imperial emotions. Recycled, mingled with History, the legend and the myth may gain nothing from such products, but the profitable existence of this market speaks for the permanence of a memory, an appeal, a dream. Furthermore, these books, often lavishly illustrated, provide a regular venue for the exhibition of the great, classic works of Napoleonic representation. They have even ventured something close to the black legend, as in *La Bataille* (1997) and *Il neigeait* (2000) by Patrick Rambaud.

Science fiction, political fiction, history-fiction! The imagination has a field day when it comes to Napoleon, that inexhaustible subject of what-if histories known as 'uchronias' or *uchronies*. What if the Emperor had been victorious at Waterloo? What if he had escaped from St. Helena? If Corsica had remained Genoese? And if . . . on and on? Among the most flavorsome examples, we should mention *La Mort de Napoléon* (1986) by Simon Leys (the historian Pierre Ryckmans) and *Le Feld-Maréchal von Bonaparte* (1996) by Jean Dutourd. Intellectual games? Harmless entertainments? Perhaps but what if there should come another dream factory who has only to write a counter-myth or imagine another legend, this time for real? Finally, the Napoleon of modern letters could not escape either caricature or parody. Ground up in the mill of irreverent or frankly risqué comedy, sent-up by the pen of a Cavanna, a Henri Viard, or a Frédéric Dard, the

Emperor finds himself back in the spot where the English caricaturists once placed him.

Let us bet that literature—popular, elitist, serious, entertaining—will never abandon such a character, so long as 'Napoleomania' of every sort continues to multiply images and objects without let. It is as if time, far from having weakened the myth, had in fact reinvigorated it—had, by force of passion, swept up many new recruits among people fascinated by the biggest of History's bigger-than-life figures.

opposite: The 19th century, all over the world, generated a great mass of publications on Napoleonic themes. Much of the literature was popular, issued in periodicals and fascicles, whether biographies, accounts of real incidents, or pure fantasy.

below: Among the what-if histories, *L'Aviateur de Bonaparte* (1926), by Jean d'Agraives, was one of the most inventive. In this fantasy the General owed his success to a flying machine that kept him continuously informed about enemy movements.

above: Postcards proved to be the medium of choice within the world of popular or industrial art. Some cards, such as the one here, were put together like puzzles, often with reproductions of key paintings illustrating the legend, but also with staged scenes.

'Napoleon is the world in summary. . . . He is a being whose arms are not long enough to embrace something larger than himself: the Revolution. Napoleon is a paroxysm in his own time, which is a paroxysm in Time. And for me the cinema is the paroxysm of life.' With these words, Abel Gance suggested the epic scale of his conception. Along the way to its realization, the film traveled a very bumpy road. In 1923 the director divided the life of the Emperor into six periods: from his youth in Corsica to the Italian campaign; from Arcola to Marengo; from 18 Brumaire to Austerlitz; from Austerlitz to the Hundred Days; Waterloo; and St. Helena. He would realize only two films dedicated to Napoleon: *Napoléon vu par Abel Gance* in 1927 and *Austerlitz* in 1960, the latter with Pierre Mondy playing the Emperor.

The complete, or 'definitive,' version of *Napoléon*, conceived for projection across three screens, was premiered in two parts at two press matinees on the 9th and 10th of May 1927. The total running time was 7 hours and 27 minutes. With the arrival of 'talkies,' Gance reworked and 'sonorized' his film, turning it into a picture with sound. Completed in 1934–1935, it ran for 140 minutes. In 1954 Gance revised and modified this version for three screens. In 1971 he reorganized his material into *Bonaparte et la Révolution*, a film 4 hours and 46 minutes in length. Subsequently, the film-maker Kevin Brownlow patiently and meticulously reconstituted a part of the original 1927 picture.

opposite: The actor Albert Dieudonné, in 1925, who played Bonaparte in Abel Gance's *Napoléon*, a role that would mark him for life.

The cinema's other great priest dedicated the Napoleonic cult was Sacha Guitry. As a principal, secondary, or cameo character, Napoleon figured in six of Guitry's films: *Les Perles de la couronne* (1937), *Remontons les Champs-Élysées* (1939), *Le Destin fabuleux de Désirée Clary* (1942), *Le Diable boiteux* (1948), *Si Versailles m'était conté* (1954), and *Napoléon* (1955).

above: In Sacha Guitry's *Napoléon* Daniel Gélin (here with the director) played Bonaparte and Raymond Pellegin Napoleon. For this work Guitry revisited the theme of providential destiny.

opposite, above: Guitry staged the coronation scene like an excerpt from David's *Sacre* (pages 64–65).

opposite, below: In Guitry's *Napoléon* Jean Gabin, despite the lack of physical resemblance, played Marshal Lannes in the moving death scene after the Battle of Essling.

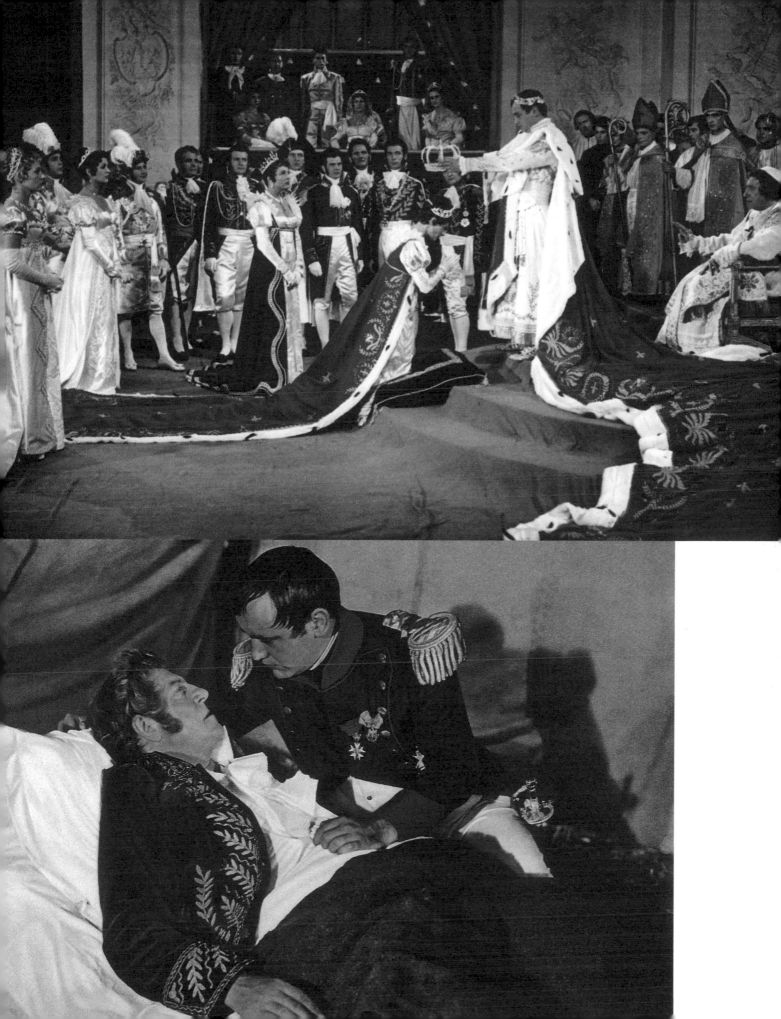

Napoleon, his life, and his times have been addressed in several hundred films. Rarely has Hollywood treated the subject and then most often fancifully. In historical productions the Emperor frequently functions as a marginal figure, but one who sometimes becomes a presence even in absence. This could be seen to telling effect in King Vidor's *War and Peace* (1957).

above, right: Karl Grüne, *Waterloo*, 1929. In this rare film the actor Charles Vanel played the hapless Emperor.

opposite and above, left: Henry Koster, *Désirée*, 1954. Hollywood's Napoleon may be a despot and an invading conqueror, but he is also a great lover. In *Désirée* Marlon Brando and Jean Simmons, Hollywood stars par excellence, played a couple torn by the contradictions of love and power, a universal and inexhaustible theme.

As the images on these pages attest, the international cinema is rich and diverse in Napoleonic material, even though the posters often revert to the iconic imagery of the legend.

left: Lupu Pick, *Napoléon à Sainte-Hélène*, 1929. Abel Gance sold his scenario for *Sainte-Hélène* in Germany, where Lupu Pick turned it into the picture advertised in this poster. The image is a stylized version of the drawing an English officer made of the Emperor on his deathbed (page 103).

opposite, above left: Leopold Savona, *Légions Impériales*. This time it was the Italians' turn at the Napoleonic story.

above and opposite, above right: Serguei Bondartchuk, *War and Peace*.

opposite, below: Joussef Chahine, *Adieu Bonaparte*.

Proof, if any were needed, that Napoleonic themes remain vital, Yves Simoneau, in 2002, directed for television a cycle of four films entitled simply *Napoléon*. Adapted by Didier Decoin from the work of Max Gallo, the series starred Christian Clavier in the title role, Isabella Rossellini as Josephine, Gérard Depardieu as Fouché, and John Malkovich as Talleyrand. These films—produced by Jean-Pierre Guérin/GMY Productions in association with Lagardère Media—were completed in seven days on a budget of more than 39 million euros. The still photographs show the opulence of the historical scenes reconstructed for the series.

Among the most spectacular manifestations of 'Napoleomania' are the re-enactments, events that mobilize whole crowds of passionate devotees. They assure the epic's ongoing presence. The movement seems to grow ever larger, even in Belgium, where the Marcheurs, a sort of folklore version of military history, continue a tradition whereby veterans of the Grand Army made sentimental return visits to the local battlegrounds. Similar commemorations are held in Eastern Europe, from Austerlitz to Leipzig and as far away as Borodino near Moscow (*above*). In France, re-enactment groups began to spring up in 1984, at the instigation of Alain Pigeard. Today 'La Grande Armée,' a French federation for historical reenactment, boasts some sixty organizations, such as the one performing at Golfe-Juan in March 2002 (*right and opposite*). Those involved are particularly concerned about the accuracy of the uniforms andequipment. Needless to say, a true exercise of memory.

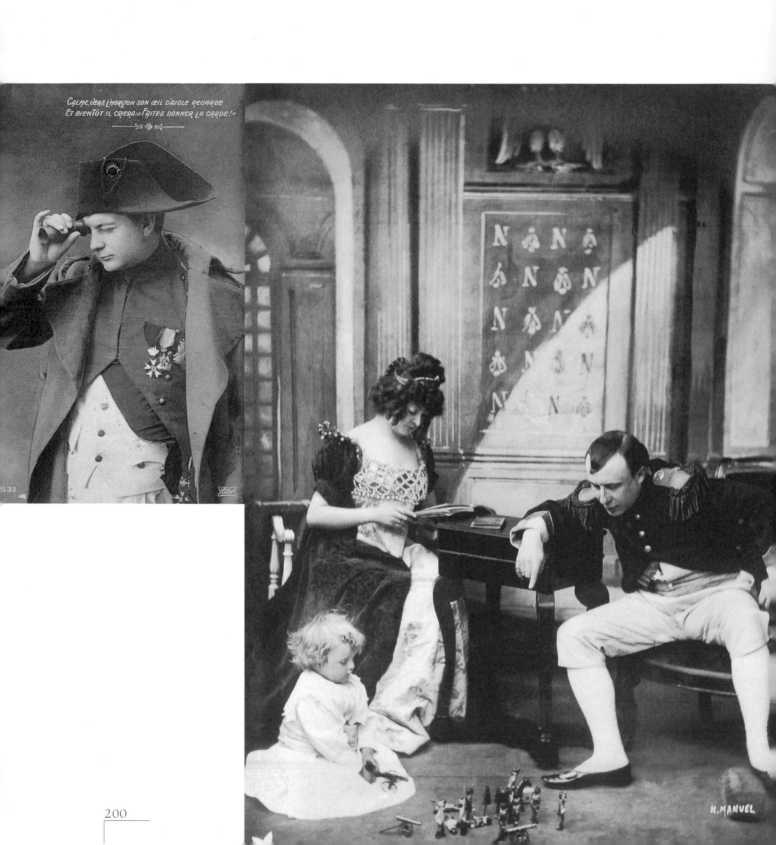

GESTES CÉLÈBRES - Napoléon embrasse le drapeau de sa garde à Fontainebleau.

opposite, left: Generally based on a painting by Horace Vernet (page 139), this postcard shows Napoleon using his spy-glass during some battle.

opposite: Napoleon as a bourgeois husband and father, with the King of Rome already playing with toy soldiers.

above, left: A grenadier seated below an air-borne Napoleon. Here the artist appears to have mistakenly based his Emperor upon an image of General Moreau as portrayed at Hohenlinden by Frédéric Henri Schopin.

right, top: Napoleon's farewell at Fontainebleau, complete with the grenadier in tears.

right, above: Children re-enacting a scene from the legend, in which the Emperor pauses to chat with one of the *braves*.

Napoleon: The Immortal Emperor

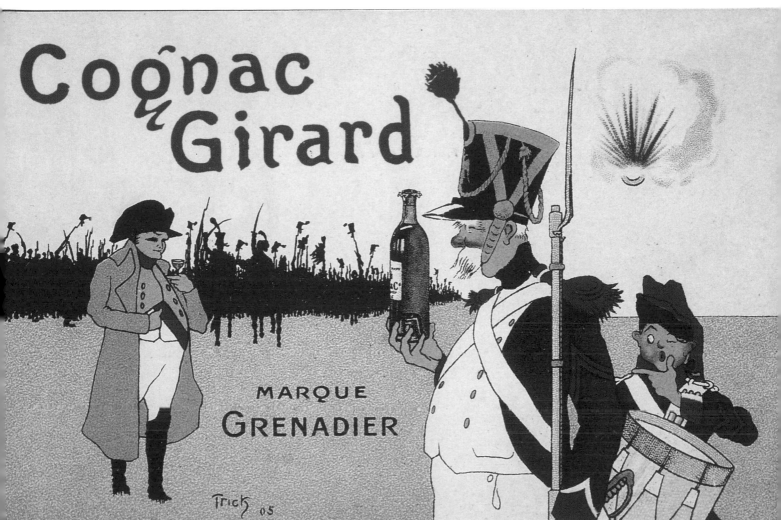

Coġnac Girard

MARQUE GRENADIER

Trick 05

DEUX GRANDS VAINQUEURS

1907 CYCLES PEUGEOT VICTOIRES EN UNE ANNÉE
TOUR DE FRANCE
G⁰ PRIX DE PARIS
CHAMPIONNAT DU MONDE
CHAMPIONNATS DE FRANCE
ROUTE et PISTE
PARIS - BRUXELLES
PARIS - ROUBAIX
PARIS - TOURS
G⁰ PRIX DES ÉTRANGERS
G⁰ PRIX AMATEURS
G⁰ PRIX DE L'U.V.F.

VICTOIRES EN DIX ANNÉES
RIVOLI
IENA
AUSTERLITZ
FRIEDLAND
WAGRAM
EYLEDT

Mich

S FILS DE PEUGEOT FRÈRES. CONSTRUCTEURS A VALENTIGNEY. (DOUBS)

There was an Empire style, which the advertising and publicity trades twisted and turned to their own advantage, as seen in these examples from the first two decades of the 20th century. Products sold under the right Napoleonic label became a kind of museum, with a big 'N' or a large eagle appearing on all manner of products: cognac, camembert, toilet water, apéritifs, vintage wines, foulards, bibelots—Napoleon atomized into endless consumer products.

AT THE HEART
of history and politics

Bonapartism, a form of authoritarian democracy, has never ceased to haunt the world. As an explicit ideology, it no longer mobilizes political forces of any significance. Nevertheless, Napoleon remained very much present in the political imagination of the 20th century. Since the publication in 1852 of Karl Marx's *The 18th Brumaire of Louis Napoleon*, the process that led from the French Revolution to the coup d'état against the Directory and then to an entirely new regime—the Empire—provides a reference point as well as a perspective from which to interpret the course of events, notably the Bolshevik revolution, which erupted in October 1917. Thus, in the debate over 'October' we find Karl Kautsky demonstrating that the Bolsheviks, being in the minority and thus unable to introduce true socialism, had no choice but to govern through a highly centralized organization and armed power. Caesarism, Bonapartism, etc.—the Napoleonic model has become a classic position in modern politics.

Since Maurice Barrès, the French right has always sought to hold up the man of energy as an exemplary figure, a model for young people. Yet Charles Maurras, a royalist, viewed all that as futile myth, and therefore dangerous, since the long cycle of war had not only cost France dearly; it also tended to embolden a foolhardy Republic. Léon Daudet, son of the great novelist Alphonse Daudet, took a classic counter-revolutionary position and denounced Napoleon as the heir of that bloody model, the French Revolution. Meanwhile, Jacques Bainville, a right-wing historian active in the prewar movement known as Action Française, revived the old theme of a savior whose time had come, simultaneously as he impugned anyone likely to lead the nation into catastrophe. The idea, though far from new, was nonetheless crucial, inasmuch as it provided a common ground not only for Bonapartists and republicans but also for the monarchist right.

Identified with France, Napoleon participated in all the great battles of the 20th century.

above: A French caricature published during the First World War. Once again Napoléon takes out his spy-glass. Clearly, France made the Emperor a welcome ally in the struggle against the Kaiser's Germany.

opposite: The victory parade held on 14 July 1919. The Arc de Triomphe, planned by Napoleon, always plays a central role in the patriotic life of France. On either side of the arch's main façade: François Rude's bas-relief entitled *La Marseillaise* and *Le Triomphe* (or *L'Apothéose*) *de Napoléon*, a relief carved by the academic master Jean-Pierre Cortot.

Napoleon, or the necessary dictator In the 20th century, an era well supplied with dictators and totalitarian regimes, this notion manifested itself in a variety of contrasting ways. In *Technique du coup d'état* (1931), Kurt Erich Suckert, better known as Curzio Malaparte (the last name derived 'Bonaparte'), analyzed the art of seizing power and paid tribute to Bonaparte, that 'European of our time,' the author of the 'first modern coup d'état.' In 1935 Mussolini, fascinated by Napoleon, inspired a play entitled *The Hundred Days*, which Giovacchino Forzano would translate into a film, *Campo di Maggio*, it too produced in 1935. And by adopting the Roman eagles as his own, Il Duce also appears to have appropriated a Napoleonic emblem. The Nazi theoretician Philipp Boulher wrote *Napoleon: The Meteoric Rise of a Genius* (1938), in which he drew a parallel between the French Emperor and Hitler: 'Many of Napoleon's ideas and acts have the same roots as those of the Führer, for a simple

reason . . . . the genius common to the two men.' All Napoleon lacked was a true political party; yet he believed it possible to establish in Europe a French Imperial hegemony of a sort that historically had belonged to the Germans. As the dictator of reference, Napoleon also became the enemy against whom the people—the nation—rose, their toughened, collective energies guided by their own charismatic leader. Just as the Stalinist cinema exalted Marshal Kutusov and the Russian people armed against the Hitler of 1812, Goebbels, even while the Reich was dying, recruited extras from the Wehrmacht, only to send them to the front the minute their work was done, so as to allow the completion of *Kolberg* (1945), a big patriotic film celebrating the heroic resistance of a small Prussian town against Napoleon's troops.

In the tumultuous and tragic history of France, the savior myth resonated broadly between 1940 and 1958. Pétain and de Gaulle—behind them

looms the profile of Napoleon. During the Occupation, French collaborators attempted, albeit in vain, to gain advantage from a new return of ashes, those of l'Aiglon, whose sarcophagus arrived from Vienna on 15 December 1940. According to historians of political ideas, Gaullism belongs in part to the Bonapartist genealogy, advocating as it does popular assembly combined with authority. Its adversaries detect Napoleonic plebiscites in the referendums, that procedure so central to the constitution of the Fifth Republic (1959–). In 1931 General de Gaulle, having conceived a certain idea of France and *la grandeur*, wrote in *La France et son armée*:

> In the presence of such a prodigious career, judgment remains divided between blame and admiration. Napoleon left France crushed, invaded, drained of blood and courage, smaller than he had found her, condemned to live with bad frontiers, the problem of which has not been solved, distrusted by Europe, a burden that, after more than a century, she still bears. But must we count for nothing the extraordinary prestige that would accrue to our strength at arms, the recognition, once and for all, accorded the [French] nation and our remarkable fighting abilities, the reputation for power that the country enjoyed and that still reverberates today?
> . . . Even in our own time . . . crowds of people, come from all over the world, pay homage to his memory and, standing close by his tomb, tremble at the grandeur of it all.

Have we now grown too small, or too cynical, or too disillusioned to assume the heritage of that grandeur. Perhaps, unless Napoleon has indeed undergone an ultimate metamorphosis, consecrated as he is by institutionalized memory, that of museums and other places of displayed learning, which may exhibit a new form of the sacred.

The Emperor may have ridiculed Wilhelm II, but he also found himself recruited into propaganda service for Vichy and French collaborators during the German occupation of France (1940–1944). Still, ever since Maurice Barrès crowned him 'professor of energy' in 1897, Napoleon has been viewed by many as a model leader in a century that was always looking for a master.

GRÂCE AUX ANGLAIS...

1939/40

NOTRE CHEMIN DE CROIX

L'ÉCOLE DE BRIENNE

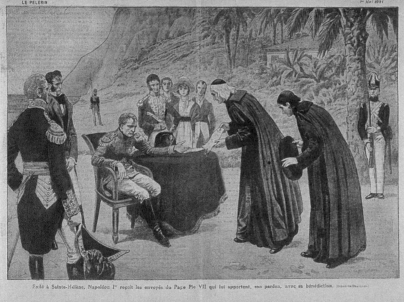

Exilé à Sainte-Hélène, Napoléon Ier reçoit les envoyés du Pape Pie VII qui lui apportent, son pardon, avec sa bénédiction.

Whatever the government in power or the historical circumstance, 20th-century France constantly looked to Napoleon. It fueled Vichyist anglophobia, rallied the nation's youth, and presented a leader before whom the powerful once bowed, even the representatives of the Pope. Most of all, it gave the country a certain image.

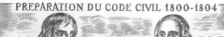

For the 10,000-franc note (type 1955), issued in 1956, the Fourth Republic decided to feature Bonaparte, in an image that Clément Serveau based upon a sketch made by David in 1797. The original plan would have had the Château de Fontainebleau represented on the verso side. However, so as not to evoke the Cour des Adieux (Farewell Courtyard), the authorities substituted the dome of the Invalides. The recto, naturally, shows the Arc de Triomphe along with the portrait.

Even today, Napoleon Bonaparte is the historical figure most often *timbrifié* or portrayed on French postage stamps, just ahead of Victor Hugo, and he even ranks high in international philately. In this field, classically enough, designers and engravers have always taken their inspiration from the great works, as did Albert Decaris in 1972 in his reinterpretation of Horace Vernet's *Bonaparte at the Arcola Bridge*, complete with the famously wrong flag (the General brandished not the tricolore but rather the banner of the 32nd demi-brigade). In 1973 it would be an excerpt from David's *Sacre*: the coronation of Josephine. For his stamp design Claude Haley used a portrait by Félix Philippoteaux and placed it next to the house in Ajaccio where the great man was born.

Monumental Napoleonic Paris includes, essentially, the Arc de Triomphe du Carrousel, the great arch at the Étoile, even though it was built during the reign of Louis-Philippe, a part of the Louvre, the Châtelet fountain, the Emperor's tomb in the crypt of the Invalides (*below and right*) and the Vendôme Column (*opposite*). Praised by Victor Hugo in 1827, in a poem that marked the writer's shift in attitude regarding Napoleon, the Vendôme Column was erected to the glory of the Grand Army, its very shaft cast in the bronze of 1,200 cannons taken from the Austrian and Russian armies. As for the urban plan, Napoleon left his mark mainly on the Rue de Rivoli, the ensemble around the Place

Le Petit Journal

LE GÉNÉRAL JAPONAIS NOGI
DEVANT LE TOMBEAU DE L'EMPEREUR AUX INVALIDES

Vendôme, and several bridges. He was also responsible for the famous sewers, the name plates at street corners, and the system of numbering houses and buildings. Yet, despite all he did for the capital, not one *place* bears his name, even though some two hundred sites commemorate the actors and victories of the Consulate and Empire. This unacceptable fact can only be explained by the vagaries of politics. Even in Luca, that charming little Italian city where Elisa Bonaparte reigned, there is a Piazza Napoleone.

THE TERRITORIES
of the sacred

We live in the age of dictionaries and encyclopedias. Thanks to the immense Napoleonic bibliography, a vast wealth of information is available to us. The 19th century found its gospel in the *Mémorial*, and we too have our bibles, such as the *Dictionnaire Napoléon*, edited by Jean Tulard (Fayard, 1987 and 1999), *Napoléon et le cinéma*, edited by Jean-Pierre Mattéi (Alain Piazzola and Cinémathèque de Corse, 1998), the *Répertoire mondial de souvenirs napoléoniens*, compiled by Alain Chappet, Roger Martin, Alain Pigeard, and André Robe (S.P.M., 1993), a quartet reminiscent of the four narrators of St. Helena. Thanks to all the above and others like them, we can make our pilgrimages without ever leaving home. Accurate, rigorous, scientific—these, overall, are the expected qualities of the modern reliquaries of history, but they apply as well to the legend. And there it is, dissected, indexed, collected. Without losing its magic, the legend has gained institutionalization.

Routes, monuments, inscriptions, documents, objects—Napoleon and the Empire have become memorial sites and the museum the repository par

right: Napoleonic museography spreads over a fascinating archipelago. The Musée de l'Armée preserves numerous mementos of the Napoleonic and Imperial wars, among them the pommel and triple scabbard of the Erfurt sword, which Napoleon carried for his meetings with Tsar Alexander in late September and early October 1808.

opposite: The Château de Malmaison, another important Napoleonic museum, contains a library that was fitted out in 1800. The desk, which came from the Tuileries, was made by the Frères Jacob.

The cultist with time to spare should put on the backpack and follow his bliss, along the Route Napoléon or Brienne or yet to the town of Wimille (Pas-de-Calais) with its Grand Army Column. Europe is once again open in every direction, all the way to Austerlitz, Leipzig, and Borodino, passing through Waterloo and Wagram. The backpacker can also sail from Elba to St. Helena. Those with a taste for uniforms should join the other Napoleonic zealots in the volunteer 'armies' that every year re-enact the great battles. So far, there is no theme park dedicated to the epic. Here is an idea whose time will surely come.

Grave scholars and fervent enthusiasts alike tramp the sacred grounds. Tourists, whether informed, passionately committed, or merely curious, will find that the Napoleonic map unfolds across the world. These travelers are keepers of the flame, sometimes without knowing it. One devotee meditates at Longwood House on St. Helena, another surveys the Waterloo battlefield and visualizes Ney's charge or the Guard's retreat, still another pauses in the Invalides crypt, turns about the camp bed preserved at the Musée de l'Armée, or strolls through the park at Malmaison. All very likely sense the wind of the epic and tremble, even if they retreat into irony so as to conceal their emotions. As for the disparagers, their very opposition gives them away as fascinated. More than with any other historical figure, it is very difficult to remain coldly objective. Even today, when everything bears us inexorably away from the kind of environment that made possible his meteoric journey, Napoleon remains, simultaneously dispersed in all manner of places and unique. Him, always him!

excellence of that memory. The man who turned the Louvre into the Musée Napoléon now finds himself parceled out among various temples, such as the Malmaison and Bois-Préau châteaux, the Napoleonic museum on the Isle of Aix, where Napoleon spent his last night on French soil, and the Bonaparte house in Ajaccio, not to mention the royal châteaux: Versailles, with its Hall of Battles, Compiègne, and Fontainebleau. In addition, there is the book/museum entitled *Histoire de Napoléon par la peinture*, edited by Jean Tulard (Belfond, 1991). The world is strewn with places for Napoleon worship, from Havana to Arenenberg (Switzerland), from New Orleans to Rome,

Needless to say, Paris still very much bears the imprint of Napoleon, from the Arc de Triomphe to the Invalides tomb, from the Vendôme Column to the Châtelet fountain, from the boulevards named for the Marshals to the Rue de Rivoli. The capital still boasts a Rue Bonaparte, but it lost the Avenue Napoléon in 1873, after it was renamed Avenue de l'Opéra. The Pont d'Iéna (Jena Bridge) survives, but not the Pont Napoléon, which became the Pont National in 1870. Pedestrians, or what the French call *flâneurs*, can relive the history of the great epic even as they make their way about Paris.

The path of Napoleon's destiny can be traced only on a map of the world.

above: Alix Daligé de Fontenay, *The Birthplace of Napoleon Bonaparte, Ajaccio, Corsica*, Château de Malmaison.

opposite: Waterloo. On the horizon looms the Butte du Lion, a cone 43 meters high and 290,000 cubic meters in volume, erected on the site where the Prince of Orange was wounded at the end of the battle. Completed in 1826, it was named for a beast that seemed to symbolize the 'victory announcing the rest that Europe won on the plains of Waterloo.'

overleaf, pages 216–217: The Emperor's library and toilet kit, Château de Malmaison. Today the places where Napoleon resided constitute repositories of memory. In 1906 Malmaison became a museum, thanks to Daniel Issla (also known as Osiris), who had bought the property in 1896. Following the death of Josephine in 1814, the château underwent numerous vicissitudes. Today the furnishings, once scattered, have been reassembled and the décor restored. The year 1800 comes closer to us with every passing day.

opposite: The campaign-tent room, Château de Fontainebleau. Between 1804 and 1814 the Emperor spent, altogether, about 150 nights at Fontainebleau, mainly to hunt.

above: Salle XIV, Château de Fontainebleau. A portrait of Pauline Bonaparte hangs on the wall. Napoleon had the château decorated, to make up for the pillage carried out during the Revolution. Pope Pius VII stayed there in 1804, while in France for the coronation, and again in 1812–1814, this time as a prisoner. In April 1814, the Emperor sought refuge at Fontainebleau, only to find himself signing his abdication there and then saying farewell to the Old Guard in the Cour du Cheval Blanc, known ever since as the Cour des Adieux (Courtyard of Farewells). Fontainebleau, which even has its own Napoleonic museum, is where one can best imagine the life of the Imperial court.

Napoleonic souvenirs run the gamut from tableware to military uniforms.

right: Sèvres plate in hard porcelain from a service made for the Tuileries (1804), Château de Fontainebleau.

opposite: The colonel of the National Guard uniform worn by Napoleon, Château de Fontainebleau.

above: This *nef* or vessel belonged to Josephine and is today preserved at Malmaison. It was made by Martin-Guillaume Biennais, a major silversmith of the period, as well as a maker of fancy objects, who delivered the piece in 1804.

opposite: Bedchamber, its bed made by Jacob-Desmalter, Compiègne. It was at Compiègne that Napoleon received Marie-Louise. He visited the château for the last time in September 1812.

left: The Empire Room in the South Wing of the Château de Versailles, furnished with pieces from the large study at the Tuileries. Napoleon did much to save Versailles and wanted to restore its brilliance.

above: An interior at the Villa des Mulini, where Napoleon resided during his reign on the Isle of Elba, from 4 May 1814 to 26 February 1815. Elba, in fact, is dense with Napoleana.

The Empire style is notable for its
military ornamentation as well as its
Classical and Egyptian motifs.
A collective creation, Empire owed its
success in large part to Vivant Denon,
the architects Percier and Fontaine, the
cabinet-makers Jacob and Séné, the
silversmiths Biennais, Auguste, and
Odiot, and the *bronzier* Pierre-Philippe
Thomire. Coherent and imperious, the
style regenerated industry and seduced
the whole of Europe.

above: An 'Athenian' washbasin made
by Pierre Benoît Marcion. This master
provided washbasins for all the Imperial
residences. The one seen here was
installed in Napoleon's bedchamber at
the Château de Compiègne.

above: Martin-Guillaume Biennais,
'Etruscan' teapot from a service made
for the Emperor.

opposite, right: Percier and Deharme,
'Egyptian' tole vase, 1804–1806.
Designed by the architect Percier and
executed by Deharme, the splendid vase
stood in Tuileries during the Empire.

left: Villa des Mulini, Isle of Elba. Corsica, Elba, St. Helena—Napoleon, in the course of his odyssey, traveled from island to island, the largest of which, England, would finally condemn him to the smallest. In little more than two years he moved from the Villa des Mulini to Longwood House on St. Helena, several thousand kilometers away. It was a fantastic period even in the life of someone who made History faster than anyone ever known.

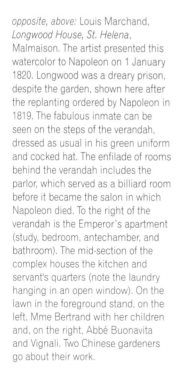

opposite, above: Louis Marchand, *Longwood House, St. Helena*, Malmaison. The artist presented this watercolor to Napoleon on 1 January 1820. Longwood was a dreary prison, despite the garden, shown here after the replanting ordered by Napoleon in 1819. The fabulous inmate can be seen on the steps of the verandah, dressed as usual in his green uniform and cocked hat. The enfilade of rooms behind the verandah includes the parlor, which served as a billiard room before it became the salon in which Napoleon died. To the right of the verandah is the Emperor's apartment (study, bedroom, antechamber, and bathroom). The mid-section of the complex houses the kitchen and servant's quarters (note the laundry hanging in an open window). On the lawn in the foreground stand, on the left, Mme Bertrand with her children and, on the right, Abbé Buonavita and Vignali. Two Chinese gardeners go about their work.

above: Longwood House viewed from the road leading to it.

opposite, below: Longwood House from another perspective.

COLLECTIONS
and auctions: the living tomb

He is everywhere. All over the world, learned societies and adulators tend the flame, in France through Les Amis du Patrimoine Napoléonien, Le Souvenir Napoléonien, La Fondation Napoléon, and the Institut Napoléon. Reviews, published in France but elsewhere as well, circulate Napoleonic scholarship, which grows apace. Several new journals have appeared just recently: *Napoléon Ier* (a bi-monthly), *Le Magazine du Consulat et de l'Empire*, and the *Revue Napoléon* (a quarterly). From internet sites (some sixty as of now, among them the remarkable napoleon.org) to tours of various physical sites associated with Napoleon, from sea voyages to St. Helena to all manner of dedicated events, such as the Mass celebrated annually on the 5th of May in the chapel under the dome of the Invalides, from performing arts (*Napoléon dévisagé* presented by the Canadian Tony Scherman in 1999), to war games, video games, and electronic games, from spectacles to television films—all attest to the shameless good health of the great man. In a further sign of vigor, there is even a controversy important enough to stir the masses: Was Napoleon poisoned? Surveys indicate that the Emperor still figures high in the French pantheon, second only to de Gaulle and ahead of Louis XIV. Napoleon continues to be a social phenomenon and a best-selling æproduct.'

The grand army of collectors Pierre-Jean Chalençon, an adept servant of the Napoleonic cause, says there are a thousand and one ways to collect and that collectors come in many forms: heir, maniac, speculator, amateur, aesthete, decorator, fetishist, conservator. The Napoleonic collector would probably have within him a bit of all these, as well as the instincts of a strategist. He must, Chalençon tells us, 'prepare, organize his plan of attack in order to take home the prize and over

time build a coherent ensemble.' Books, porcelains, snuffboxes, clothing—no matter. Each collector—carried away, like all the others, by the energy of his passion—remains one of a kind, because every hoarder of Napoleonalia goes about it in his own unique way.

Once the Eagle fell, his enemies became the first big collectors of Napoleonic souvenirs and memorabilia, beginning with the English— Wellington, Rosebery, and Mme Tussaud. (In 1923, alas, much of what Mme Tussaud had collected went up in flames, including the berlin from St. Helena.) Then came the members of the Imperial family, such as Anatole Demidoff, the husband of Princess Mathilde (the daughter of Napoleon's brother Jérôme), whose collection would form the nucleus of the San Donato Museum on the Isle of Elba. Next it was the turn of dedicated scholars, among them Frédéric Masson, who would bequeath his treasures to the Institut de France, and Prince Mikhailovitch in Russia.

The 20th century brought new competition among collectors, this time with the pace set by self-made men, autodidacts, captains of industry, CEOs, and men of power fascinated by France's great man: Prince Rainier II of Monaco; Lobau in Cuba, who, in 1959, saw his holdings nationalized, collector to survive; Martial Lapeyre, who would make a substantial gift to the Fondation Napoléon; the Prefect Milliat, whose treasures were to be dispersed at a Drouot auction; Ben Weider, the Canadian fitness king; the Japanese Ikeda, who would enrich the Fuji Museum; the Americans Malcolm Forbes and Bill Gates; and even an Australian Prime Minister, with a passion for vermeils and clocks. Other important collectors include Sacha Guitry, that great artist who did so much for the Napoleonic legend, and several statesmen: François Mitterand, who helped with the restoration of St. Helena; Dominique de Villepin, and Philippe Seguin. For many of these, the issue was one of preservation, of leaving a trace, and instead of dispersing their collections, they gave them to museums. Among the beneficiaries of their largesse have been the Musée Naval at Juan-les-Pins and the Musée Municipal of Fontainebleau. While some contemporary enthusiasts focus on militaria, among them Henry Lachouque, the modern collector is typically a family man between the ages of thirty and forty with a comfortable income, an understanding wife, an interest in objets d'art, which he views as good investments, and a sense of the cachet gained from making his passion known. Today, the collections in the hands descendants of great families are vanishing, with the exception of those owned by the Oudinots and the Massénas. Important donations were made by the Murats and Prince and Princess Napoléon. In any event, 'Napoleomania' has a bright future ahead of it. A superhero even in China (in 2002 an exhibition in Taipei drew 450,000 visitors), a nation he prophesied would astound the world once she wakes up, Napoleon has conquered the whole world.

opposite: Russian school, *Napoleon during the Russian Campaign*, c. 1830, private collection. Winter cold in late 1812 obliged the Emperor to don a fur-trimmed cloak.

left and below: Silver goblet and flatware made by Biennais and Berger, with a linen serviette (private collection).

Such price passion Since 1982 and the laws governing gifts and pre-emptions, the Louvre and museums such as Malmaison and Bois-Préau have joined the fray, which makes the market all the more rarefied. Still, there are magnificent and well-attended sales. They began as far back as 1823, when Sotheby's auctioned off the library Napoleon had accumulated on St. Helena. Next the relics changed hands bit by bit. Following the Demidoff sale at the end of the 19th century there would be a number of important auctions, such as that for the library of Marie-Louise, acquired in 1933 by Mr. and Mrs. John Jaffé, an Irish couple resident in Nice, who then presented it to Malmaison. In 1935–1937 Drouot and London auctioned off the Brower collection, which resulted in its dispersal. After World War II many of the ensembles belonging to the descendants of generals and marshals or to Prince Napoleon were sold, notably the one amassed by Bertrand. Then came the Calvin Bullock sale, conducted by Christie's in 1985.

Prices continue to climb. In 1969, during a voyage to St. Helena on the SS *France*, Moët et Chandon paid a record price for a hat hammered down by the famous auctioneer Maurice Rheims.

The sheer prodigiousness of the Imperial decade can be rediscovered in the fine and decorative arts alike, in both handsome accessories and idealized symbols.

above: A cushion made by Picot for the coronation in 1804 (private collection).

opposite: Antoine-Denis Chaudet, *Portrait Bust of Napoleon*, private collection. Porcelain from the Manufacture Impériale de Sèvres with a crown of gilt-bronze laurel made by Pierre-Philippe Thomire.

right: Book embroidered with the Emperor's large armorial bearings (private collection).

Thereafter it would cost from 75,000 to 150,000 euros to place such a relic in one's shrine. Today there are frequent sales of Napoleonic militaria, unlike the sales of mementos and decorative objects, which are more rare. Two worth mentioning are the Fontainebleau auction held on 9 March 2002, which totaled 1,500,000 euros, and the sale at Christie's eleven days later. Every twenty or twenty-five years the same items reappear, which means that several large collections will surely come on the market one day, like those of Lachouque and the Imperial family. Yet, whereas at the beginning of the 20th century a large sale required four or five catalogues, today only one catalogue suffices, with a paltry list of forty or fifty pieces. This, as well as the sums involved, explains the number of fakes now in circulation and the need for rigorous provenance.

Love having no price, the myth may not economize when it comes to authenticity. Here then is one of History's delicious ironies. The maestro of propaganda becomes the object of insatiable curiosity and the subject of countless investigations, all driven, even haunted by the question of truth. And was it not he who declared in 1815: 'The lie passes; the truth remains'?

THE PRICE OF MYTH

Towards the end of the 1990s the market heated up considerably, despite the rather mediocre quality of the pieces on offer. The observance of the bi-centenary (beginning in 1996 with the anniversary of the Italian campaign), the publication of works on the period, the organization of colloquiums—in brief, the mediatization of Napoleomania—all played a role. To be sure, several collections came up for sale, resulting in dispersal, and all historic mementos fetched good prices; still, the items of museum quality were few and far between. By this time it would have been difficult to imagine the sales of the 1930s or even the 1940s, in which quantity was virtually synonymous with quality and good provenance. The arrival of many new, well-heeled collectors could only cause further decline in the Napoleonic art market. These late-comers appeared ready to pay any price for whatever object they coveted. In 2000 one of the Emperor's silver campaign plates went for the equivalent of 35,000 euros, once hammered down at Trajan's. The new millennium will no doubt bring all sorts of change, and the madness of the market has yet to run its course. P.-J. C.

opposite, above: Handkerchiefs once owned by Napoleon (private collection).

opposite, below: Antonio Canova, *Medallion Portrait of Napoleon*, private collection.

above: Signet ring and snuffbox once owned by Napoleon (private collection). In 1810 the Emperor gave the ring to a high dignitary at the Dutch court.

below: A red-velvet sleeve from one of the frockcoats worn by the First Consul (private collection). Stained in the course of a dinner, it was unstitched and saved by Chevallier, Napoleon's tailor. The coat itself disappeared in 1815.

THE EMPEROR'S PERSONAL OBJECTS

Hammer prices from recent sales in equivalent
 euros

Hat: 150,000 euros

Campaign bed: 80,000–100,000 euros

Lock of hair: 4,000–8,000 euros

Handkerchief: 10,000–15,000 euros

Vermeil pitcher: 150,000 euros

Book emblazoned with the arms of Napoleon:
 15,000–20,000 euros

Flatware place-setting made by Biennais:
 15,000–20,000 euros

NAPOLEONIC MEMENTOS

Watch once owned by Marie-Louise:
 50,000–60,000 euros

Baton of a First Empire marshal: 80,000–
 120,000 euros

Saber once owned by Murad Bey: 200,000 euros

Marble bust of Jérôme Bonaparte: 12,000 euros

Frockcoat of a Councilor of State (1804 model):
 30,000 euros

Sèvres vase given by Napoleon to Talleyrand:
 80,000 euros

top: A box made of gold and tortoise shell in c. 1810 and once owned by Pauline Borghese, Napoleon's youngest sister (private collection).

left: Plate from a dessert service (c. 1810) formerly owned by Charles Maurice de Talleyrand-Périgord (private collection).

Porcelains, portraits, bibelots—the Imperial era seems to unfold as little more than a Prévert inventory. Still, every object is endowed with added value beyond all measure: the dream of which it is a concentrated form.

right: Officer's shako, model 1812 (private collection).

opposite, top: Henri-Robert Riesener, *Portrait of Mlle Bourgoin*, private collection. This actress, celebrated for her performances at the Comédie Française, was the mistress of both Napoleon and Tsar Alexander I, among others.

opposite, below right: Milk pitcher made by the Manufacture de Sèvres and delivered to Napoleon on 1 January 1805 (private collection).

opposite, below left: Plaster cast of the King of Rome's right hand made in c. 1813–1814 and once owned by Dubois, 'midwife' to Marie-Louise (private collection).

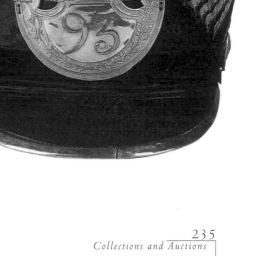

Napoleonic relics, inanimate though they may be, seem imbued with the immortality of the meteor who illuminated his century.

above and right: A copy of the *Cérémonial de l'Empire français* (1809) that once belonged to Napoleon

opposite, above: Jean-Baptiste Isabey, *Preparatory Study: The Visit of the Consul to the Sevenné Cotton Factory*, 1802, private collection. See the final drawing on page 55.

opposite, left: Lotto gaming box made for Napoleon by Biennais, from the Château de Fontainebleau (private collection).

opposite, right: Antoine-Denis Chaudet, *Bust of Napoleon*, Empire period, bronze, private collection.

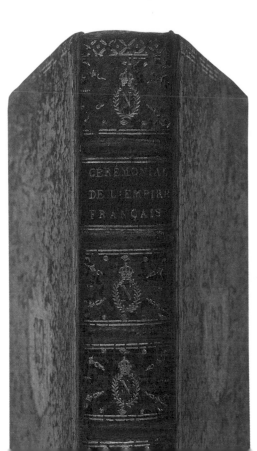

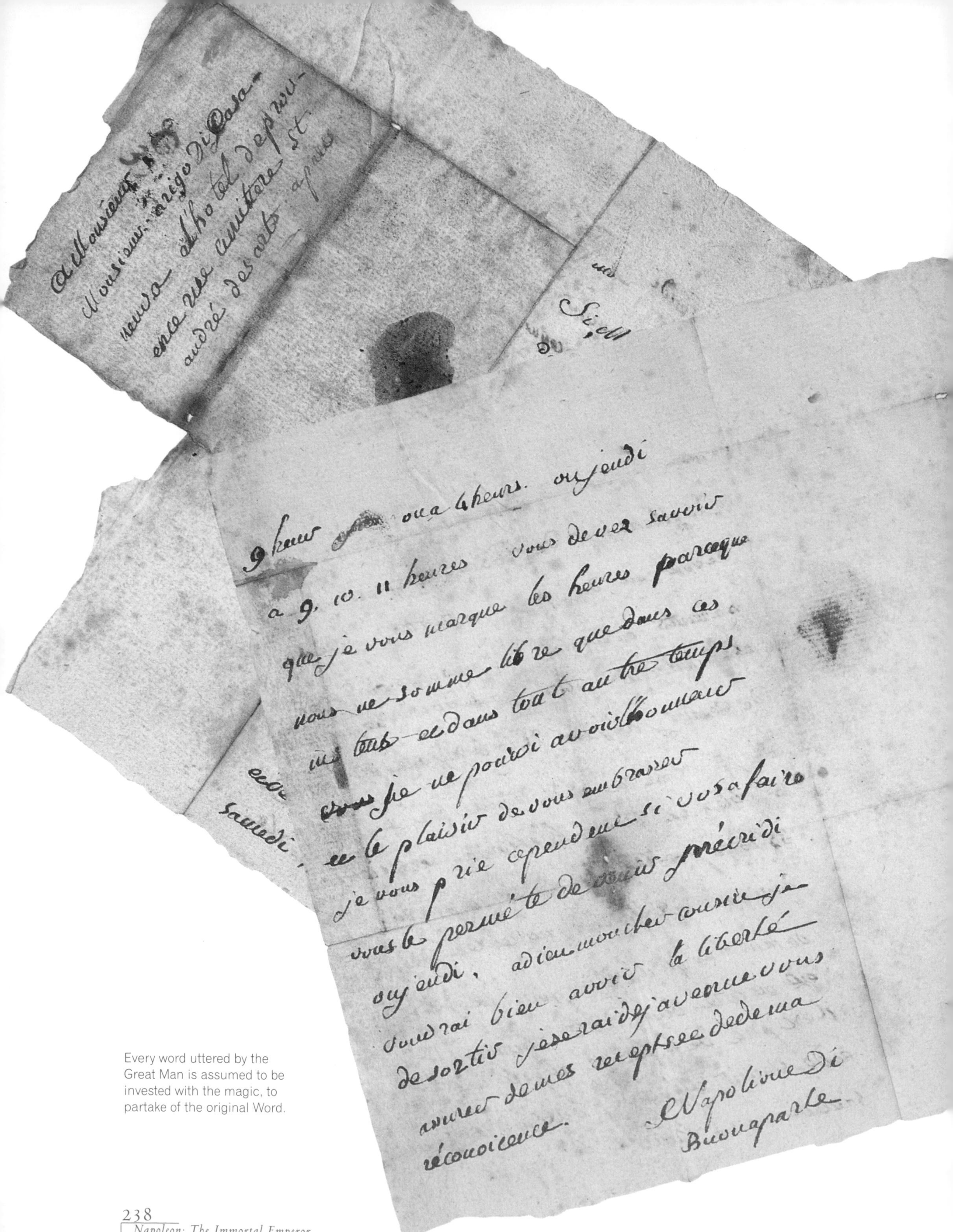

A Monsieur
Monsieur Arrigo Di Casanova
à l'hotel de provence rue cimitiere St.
andré des arts a paris

9 heur ou a 6 heurs. ou jeudi
a 9. 10. 11 heures vous devez savoir
que je vous marque les heures parceque
nous ne somme libre que dans ces
ces tems et dans tout autre temps
vous je ne pourroi avoir l'honneur
et le plaisir de vous embrasser
je vous prie cependant si vos affaire
vous le permette de venir mecredi
ou jeudi. adieu mon cher ami je
voudrai bien avoir la liberté
de sortir je serai deja venu vous
assurer de mes respects et de ma
réconoissance. Napolione di
Buonaparte

Every word uttered by the Great Man is assumed to be invested with the magic, to partake of the original Word.

above: The order, signed by Napoleon in 1798, to have the leaders of the Cairo revolt buried (private collection).

On the collectors' market, a letter signed by Napoleon may fetch between 800 and 10,000 euros. A letter written in his own hand sells for between 10,000 and 300,000 euros.

opposite: A letter hand-written and signed by Bonaparte at the age of fifteen (private collection). In it the author describes, for his cousin, father of the future Duke of Padua, his activities at the École Militaire in Paris.

overleaf, page 240: Two-page codicil that Napoleon wrote out by hand and signed for addition to his will (private collection). This is a more personal and moving document than the will he had dictated to Montholon and then spent five hours copying in mid-April 1821.

...tout ce que vous pourrez pour
... un jour. Les
... nos ... des
... les biens que j'ai été ... ici.

Je vous remercie ...
... avec ...
... d'une ... 6 personnes.

Gardez tout cela ...
me les rendre si ...

Fait ...

Neveu   Roland

Lenoire   Mérimée   Peyron

Baltard   Chaudet

Moreau   Allais   De Thière David   Girard

Dejer   Blot

Berthelemy   Monget

Julien   Thibault   Naigeon Aué   Hamey Bervic

LeBrun   Ch. Bienaimé

Commissaire Expert du Musée

Espercieux   Carle Vernet

Reynault   Moitte   Vien

Saintaubin   Auguste   Meynier

Alex.dre Tardieu   Fragonard   Redouté   Durand

Anselin   Morel

Manard   Prud'hon   P.F. L. Fontaine

Langlois

Napoleon bought all his hats from Poupard et Cie, which charged 60 francs a piece, a price the Emperor was always trying to negotiate down. The surviving Imperial hats illustrated on this page all belong to private collectors.

NAPOLEON'S HAT

It was apparently during the Consulate period that Napoleon definitively adopted the very simple hat that rapidly became legendary. Napoleon's hats have no stripes around the edge, and their button is covered in woven horsehair or black silk, all quite different from the model of officer's hat required since 1786, with its black border stripe and gilt or silver-gilt button. It has long been established, virtually by religious tenet, that Napoleon's personal headwear should be designated as the 'little hat.' Between 1801 and 1804 the First Consul chose a model that could be worn with any uniform regardless of the buttons on it. The portraits of Napoleon by Isabey and Meissonier show the formal evolution of the 'little hat' from the Peace of Amiens (1802) to the French Campaign (1814). The thickness of the felt is not always the same. Indeed, some of the hats are made of very light felt. The cockade also underwent modifications in the course of time. How many hats could the 'Temple of Taste' (the shop owned by the hatmaker Poupard) have supplied to the First Consul and then the Emperor?

It was at least three hats every quarter, making total of 168 worn and discarded between 1802 and 1815. After all, these *coiffures* were relatively fragile, and a single journey in the rain would have left a felt hat hopelessly out of shape. How many have survived? About twenty? Perhaps a few more? This small number should not surprise, given that M. Gervais, director of the Imperial wardrobe, agreed to pass on Napoleon's hats to his launderer, who turned them into 'grips' used for working with hot irons. Luckily for collectors and museums, other members of the household staff treated the Emperor's clothing less off-handedly. In the 1930s one of Napoleon's little hats was sold at Drouot for 354,000 old francs. More recently, in 1970, 1973, and 1975, three Imperial hats sold privately fetched between 125,000 and 180,000 francs. In 1998 a hat was put up for sale on the Paris market at a price of more than 1 million francs. Today three or four hats remain in private collections; all the others are now in museums. P.-J. C.

AT THE DAWN
of the third millennium

*I feel
the infinite
within me.*
Napoleon Bonaparte,
1800

'The man of genius is a meteor destined to burn out in order to illuminate his century.' With these powerful words, uttered in Lyons in the year 1800, the First Consul illuminates even now in the third millennium. They understood it perfectly well, those grenadiers extolled by Henrich Heine, the soldiers painted by Detaille, those peasants of Balzac being told the story of the great man: Napoleon is immortal. It remains only for us to question that immortality. Humanity still has the need to dream, to admire, to become involved, at least for the time it takes to explore a Napoleonic site, to read a book or play a game. In terms of image, who could rival the Emperor? Of course, our era has had its share of figures with front-page familiarity all over the world. A certain moustache, a certain beret, a certain cigar—all have had and still possess a quasi-universal iconic value, for better or for worse. None of them enjoys or, we bet, will ever enjoy the kind of staying power known by Napoleon.

Owner of the whole world, Napoleon also owns the historians. This leap across the lands of legend, which will be completed as soon as you turn the last page of the book in hand, would have been impossible without their remarkable works, vampired for the occasion. Monuments such as Jean Tulard's *Le Mythe de Napoléon* (1971) and *Napoléon ou le Mythe du sauveur* (1977), Natalie Petiteau's *Napoléon, de la mythologie à l'histoire* (1999), and Annie Jourdan's *Napoléon, héros, imperator, mécène* (1998) make available to us all that is important in present-day scholarship. But let us also acknowledge their distinguished precursors, such as Charles Chassé and his *Napoléon par les écrivains*, published in 1921.

Do not doubt it: the 21st century will be Napoleonic. The power of the imagination in tandem with accurate historical knowledge guarantees the survival or the perpetual renascence of the victor of Austerlitz and the vanquished of Waterloo. A man, nothing but a man, of course. But the Invisible was perhaps there for something . . . . *Chi lo sa?*

opposite: Antonio Canova, *The Emperor Napoleon I*, c. 1808, gouache, private collection. The face of Napoleon in the guise of a Roman emperor, which also evokes the features of Alexander the Great, seems to embody the very essence of Neoclassicism.

APPENDICES

Chronology

1769
15 AUGUST: Napoleone Buonaparte born in Ajaccio, Corsica, the second son of Charles Buonaparte and Letizia Romalino.

1771
21 JULY: Baptism in Ajaccio Cathedral by his great-uncle, Archdeacon Lucien.

1778
15 DECEMBER: He leaves for the Continent with his older brother Joseph to accompany his father, appointed deputy for the nobility at the Estates-General on the side of the King.

1779
15 MAY: Enters the military school at Brienne. The snowball battle invented by Bourienne and filmed by Abel Gance (1927) would have occurred during the winter of 1783.

1784
22 OCTOBER: Enters the École Militaire in Paris.

1785
28 SEPTEMBER: Made Second Lieutenant.

3 NOVEMBER: Joins the regiment of La Fère at Valence.

1786
15 SEPTEMBER: Granted his first leave allowing him to return to Corsica, where he remains a year.

1788
JANUARY–MAY: Second stay in Corsica.
JUNE: Garrisoned at Auxonne.

1789
1 APRIL: Helps to quell a riot in Seurre.
23 AUGUST: Oath of loyalty to the Nation, the King, and the Law.
30 OCTOBER: Leaves for Corsica, where he takes active part in the projects and political activism of the patriotic clubs.

1790
Spends the year in Corsica; attempts to ingratiate himself with Paoli, who keeps the Buonapartes at arm's length.

1791
Returns to the Continent in February. Attends the meetings of the Jacobins in Valence; announces his support for the Republic. *La Lettre à Buttafuoco*. Back to Corsica in the autumn.

1792
On the Continent in May. Visits Paris and takes part in the events of 20 June–10 August. Made Captain in July, he returns to Corsica in October.

1793
FEBRUARY: As head of the Corsican volunteers, he seizes the island of Santo Stefano, Sardinia.
MARCH–JUNE: Rupture with Paoli; decree of accusation from the Convention. Following a short stay on the Continent, he returns to Corisca with a Republican army to put down a revolt by Paoli supporters. The effort fails, and the Buonapartes leave the island.
29 JULY: Publication of *Le Souper de Beaucaire*, a political dialogue in which he sides with the Convention.
16 SEPTEMBER: Appointed head of the artillery attempting to break the siege of Toulon. The port retaken from the English on 19 December.

22 DECEMBER: Made Brigadier General.

1794
JANUARY: *La Prise de Toulon* ('a patriotic deed') performed on the Paris stage.
FEBRUARY–JULY: Takes part in several military operations in Northern Italy.
9 AUGUST: Arrested as a Robespierrist, he nonetheless escapes the Thermidor purge and is released on 20 August.

1795
21 APRIL: Engaged to Désirée Clary.
13 JUNE: Appointed to the Army of the West. Has himself placed on leave.
18 AUGUST: Appointed to the topophial (map-making) office of the War Ministry.
15 SEPTEMBER: Crossed off the list of generals employed by the Committee of Public Safety. Period of financial difficulties.
5 OCTOBER: Takes part in the events of 13 Vendémiare and becomes known as 'General Vendémiare,' thanks to his rout of the Royalists assembled on the steps of Saint-Roche Church in Paris.
11 OCTOBER: At the Convention Fréron mentions his name.
15 OCTOBER: Meets Josephine de Beauharnais.
26 OCTOBER: Appointed Commanding General of the Army of the Interior, which quickly makes him known as 'General Police.'

1796
2 MARCH: Appointed Commanding General of the Army of Italy.
9 MARCH: Marries Josephine de Beauharnais, witnessed by Barras and Tallien.
APRIL: The Italian campaign begins.
APRIL–NOVEMBER: Victories at Montenotte (12 April), Millesmo

(13 April), Dego (15 April), Mondovi (21 April), Lodi (10 May), Lonato (3 August), Castiglione (5 August), Roveredo (4 September), Bassano (8 September), Saint-Georges (15 September), and Arcola (15–17 Novmber).

After the capture of the Lodi bridge, an event that would be re-enacted on the Paris stage, the soldiers in the Army of Italy nickname Bonaparte 'the Little Corporal.'

1797

14 JANUARY: Rivoli victory.
2 FEBRURY: Fall of Mantua.
18 APRIL: Preliminary peace talks with the Austrians, held at Loeben.
4 SEPTEMBER: The coup d'état of 18 Fructidor. Sends Augereau to support the Directory.
17 OCTOBER: Peace of Campoformio.
25 DECEMBER: Elected to the Institut de France.

From May 1796 until December 1797, the Commanding General of the Army of Italy proved masterful in the management of his own propaganda. After the Arcola bridge episode, completely transformed by the legend, the treaty of Campoformio and the election to the Institut de France took Bonaparte's early prestige to its culminating moments.

1798

12 APRIL: Appointed Commander of the Army of the Orient.
19 MAY: The French fleet sets sail for Egypt. Beginning in May, the propaganda machine linked to the Egyptian expedition is in full operation.
11 JUNE: Malta occupied.
1 JULY: Disembarkation near Alexandria. Start of the Egyptian campaign. Victories: Chebrets (13 July) and Pyramids (21 July).
1 AUGUST: The French fleet destroyed by the English navy at Aboukir.
22 AUGUST: Creation of the Institut d'Egypte.
OCTOBER: Desaix'ss conquest of Upper Egypt. Revolt in Cairo on the 21st.

1799

Syrian campaign. Capture of El-Arich (20 February) and Jaffa (7 March). Defeat before Saint-Jean-d'Acre (March–May). Victory at Mont-Thabor (16 April). Syria evacuated.
25 JULY: Victory at Aboukir.
23 AUGUST: Departure for France.
16 OCTOBER: Arrival in Paris.
9–10 NOVEMBER: Coup d'état of 18 Brumaire, the episode magnified by propaganda. A commissioned engraving disseminates the official version of the Saint-Cloud event.
15 DECEMBER: The Consulate proclaimed; Bonaparte (First Consul), Cambarcérès, and Lebrun in charge of the new government.

In 1799 French royalists begin to publish caricatures ridiculing the First Consul. The English also lampoon first Bonaparte, then Napoleon, and finally both Consular and Imperial France. Many more send-ups would follow, everywhere Europe.

1800

13 FEBRUARY: Creation of the Banque de France.
17 FEBUARY: Law governing the administrative organization of France.
19 FEBRUARY: The First Consul moves into the Tuileries, cause for a whole new level of symbolism.
MAY–JUNE: The second Italian campaign. Victory at Marengo (14 June). The campaign takes a legendary turn when the First Consul leads his army across the Great St. Bernard Pass, an episode painted by David.
2 JUILLET: The Parisian populace greets the First Consul in triumph.
2 OCTOBER: Treaty of Mortefontaine signed with the United States.
24 OCTOBER: Failure of the 'dagger conspiracy' against Bonaparte.
1 NOVEMBER: Publication of Fontane's *Parallèle entre César, Cromwell, Monk et Bonaparte*, a political pamphlet encouraged by Lucien Bonaparte.
3 DECEMBER: Moreau's victory at Hohenlinden.
24 DECEMBER: Assassination attempt upon Bonaparte in Rue Saint-Niçaise.

1801

9 FEBRUARY: Peace of Lunéville signed with Austria.
29 MARCH: Peace of Florence signed with the Kingdom of Naples.
15 JULY: Signing of the Concordat with the Vatican, preceded by the Church's participation in the national celebration of 14 July.
8 OCTOBER: Peace of Paris signed with Russia.

1802

25 MARCH: Peace of Amiens signed with England.
26 APRIL: Amnesty for émigrés.
10 MAY: Plebiscite proposing that Napoleon Bonaparte be made Consul for Life, the name Napoleon used in an official context for the first time.
19 MAY: The Legion of Honor created.
20 MAY: Slavery re-established in the French colonies.
25 JULY: Peace with the Ottoman Empire.
2 AUGUST: Napoleon named Consul for Life.

Fueled by propaganda, the legend is henceforth well embedded. Brumaire renders the savior and statesman myth all the more credible. At the Salon of 1802 Isabey exhibits his *Bonaparte at Malmaison*, a painting that immortalizes the image of Napoleon with his little hat and one hand slipped into his vest.

1803

30 APRIL: Napoleon sells France's Louisiana Territory to the United States. For a price of three cents per acre, the U.S doubles its size, acquiring land now occupied by thirteen states west of the Mississippi, from Canada to New Orleans.

1804

FEBRUARY–MARCH: Arrest and execution of the royalist conspirators. Exile of Moreau. The Duc d'Enghien seized and executed on 20–21 March.
21 MARCH: The Civil Code introduced.
18 MAY: The Empire proclaimed. Eighteen Marshals of France appointed. Court etiquette re-established.

15 JULY: Napoleon receives the first insignia—the 'eagle'—of the Legion of Honor.

2 DECEMBER: Coronation of Napoleon in Notre-Dame de Paris, the ceremony steeped in elaborate symbolism, derived from both the Bourbons and ancient Merovigian and Carolingian models. Thus, bees embroidered in gold proliferate on the purple mantles worn by Napoleon and Josephine as well as on the tapestries hung in the cathedral nave. David's huge canvas (*Le Sacre*) commemorating the scene exhibited at the Salon of 1808. Imperial propaganda picks up where the Consular left off.

5 DECEMBER: The first distribution of eagles.

In 1804 British pamphleteers give birth to the 'dark legend.' The ogre theme appears. At the Salon Carle Vernet exhibits his *Battle of Marengo*, the First Consul at the center of the action. After a *senatus consultum* names Napoleon Emperor, Beethoven retitles his Third Symphony, calling it the *Eroica* rather than the *Bonaparte* as originally planned.

1805

26 MARCH: Napoleon crowned King of Italy.

APRIL–AUGUST: The third coalition against France: Russia, Austria, and Naples.

1 OCTOBER: Victory at Elchingen

7 OCTOBER: Publication of the first *Bulletin de la Grande Armée*.

20 OCTOBER: Capitulation of Ulm.

21 OCTOBER: Battle of Trafalgar; the English navy destroys the French fleet but loses Admiral Lord Nelson.

14 NOVEMBER: Entrance of Napoleon into Vienna.

2 DECEMBER: Victory at Austerlitz.

26 DECEMBER: The Treaty of Presburg signed with Austria.

The 14th of August becomes the feast day of Saint Napoleon, then a national holiday in 1806. Lebrun publishes his 'Ode à la Grande Armée,' one of countless poems dedicated to the glory of the Emperor and the Empire.

1806

1 JANUARY: The Gregorian calendar restored.

15 MARCH: Murat becomes the Grand Duke of Berg.

30 MARCH: Joseph Bonaparte becomes King of Naples.

4 APRIL: The *Imperial Catechism* is published.

10 MAY: Imperial University created.

5 JULY: Louis Bonaparte becomes King of Holland.

12 JULY: Napoleon protector of the Confederation of the Rhine. The fourth coalition forms: England, Prussia, Russia, and Saxony.

JULY–OCTOBER: Prussian campaign. Victories at Jena and Auerstaedt (14 October). Berlin occupied (17 October).

21 NOVEMBER: Start of the Continental Blockade.

1807

JANUARY–FEBRUARY: Campaign in Poland (Napoleon meets Marie Walewska on 1 January). The Battle of Eylau (8 February).

14 JUNE: Victory at Friedland.

25 JUNE: Treaty of Tilsit; Napoleon and Tsar Alexander I meet.

22 JULY: Grand Duchy of Warsaw created.

9 AUGUST: Talleyrand removed from the Ministry of Exterior Relations.

16 AUGUST: Jérôme Bonaparte becomes King of Westphalia.

16 SEPTEMBER: Cour des Comptes (Government Accounting Office) created.

OCTOBER–NOVEMBER: Junot's campaign in Portugal.

1808

2 FEBRUARY: Rome occupied.

1 MARCH: Imperial nobility created.

APRIL–JULY: Intervention in the affairs of Spain. Joseph Bonaparte named King of Spain. Defeat at Bailén (22 July). Murat becomes King of Naples.

30 AUGUST: French capitulation at Cintra in Portugal.

NOVEMBER: Spanish campaign. Napoleon's victory at Somo-Sierra.

20 DECEMBER: Fouché and Talleyrand reconcile in preparation for the future in the event Napoleon should disappear.

1809

Fifth coalition: Great Britain and Austria.

22 APRIL: Victory at Eckmühl.

13 MAY: Vienna taken.

22 MAY: Battle of Essling.

10 JUNE: Pius VII excommunicates Napoleon.

5–6 JULY: Victory at Wagram. Austria seeks an armistice.

7 JULY: Pope Pius VII is arrested.

14 OCTOBER: Treaty of Vienna.

DECEMBER: Napoleon divorces Josephine.

1810

17 FEBRUARY: Rome becomes part of the Empire.

1–2 APRIL: Napoleon and Marie-Louise are married.

3 JUNE: Fouché disgraced.

9 JULY: Holland annexed.

21 AUGUST: Bernadotte elected Prince Royal of Sweden.

13 DECEMBER: After the annexation of the Hanseatic cities, Imperial France comprises 130 departments.

1811

20 MARCH: The birth of the King of Rome, baptized on 9 June. Delavigne publishes 'Dithyrambe sur la naissance du roi de Rome,' one of many poems composed to mark the occasion.

1812

19 JANUARY: The beginning of Wellington's victories in Spain.

JUNE–DECEMBER: Russian campaign. Vilna taken (28 June) followed by Smolensk (17 August). Victory at the Moskova (7 September). Entrance into Moscow (14 September). The French retreat begins (18 October). The Berezina crossed (25–28 November).

23 OCTOBER: In Paris, General Malet attempts a coup d'état.

5 DECEMBER: Napoleon leaves the Grand Army and sets off for Paris.

18 DECEMBER: Napoleon arrives in Paris. At the Salon d'Autumn Horace

Vernet exhibits *The Capture of an Entrenched Camp*, his first picture seen there.

1813

Sixth coalition (England, Austria, Prussia, Russia, and Sweden).
MAY–OCTOBER: German campaign. Victories at Lützen (2 May), Bautzen (20 May), Dresden (26–27 August). French defeat at Leipzig (16–19 October). Victory at Hanau (30 October). Spain falls to the Allies (21 June), followed by Holland (16 November).

1814

17 JANUARY: Murat defects. The coalition attacks the French at home as well as everywhere else in Europe, with the exception of Denmark and Turkey.

29 JANUARY: Victory at Brienne.
1 FEBRUARY: Defeat at La Rothière.
FEBRUARY–MARCH: Victories at Champaubert (10 February), Montmirail (11), Château-Thierry (12), Vauchamp (13), Montereau (18). Indecisive battles at Craonne (7 March) and Laon (9). Victory at Rheims (13). Defeat at Arcis-sur-Aube (20).
31 MARCH: The Allies enter Paris.
2 APRIL: The French Senate declares Napoleon dethroned.
4 APRIL: Napoleon abdicates, then unconditionally on the 6th. The Senate summons Louis XVIII.
11 APRIL: Treaty of Fontainebleau; Napoleon given sovereignty over Elba.
20 APRIL: Napoleon says farewell at Fontainebleau and departs for Elba.
30 MAY: Treaty of Paris.
4 JUNE: Constitutional charter promulgated by Louis XVIII. The first Restoration.
SEPTEMBER: Congress of Vienna opens.

1814

An important new historiography comes into play, this time anti-Napoleonic. At the beginning of the year Benjamin Constant publishes *De l'esprit de comquête et de l'usurpation*. Byron, hostile to the Emperor, writes his 'Ode to Napoleon.' On April 5

Chateaubriand publishes his *De Bonaparte et des Bourbons*. In May begins the clandestine spread of images and symbols prohibited by the Restoration.

1815

26 FEBRUARY: Napoleon leaves Elba.
1 MARCH: Lands at Golfe-Juan.
20 MARCH: Arrives at the Tuileries.
22 APRIL: *Acte additionnel* becomes part of the Constitutions of the Empire. Seventh coalition (England, Austria, Prussia, Russia, Sweden, and virtually the rest of Europe).
9 JUNE: Congress of Vienna adjourns.
15 JUNE: The French cross into Belgium.
16 JUNE: Victory at Ligne.
18 JUNE: The Battle of Waterloo.
22 JUNE: Napoleon abdicates.
8 JULY: Louis XVIII returns to Paris. The Second Restoration.
15 JULY: Napoleon surrenders to the English.
16 OCTOBER: Arrival at St. Helena.
20 NOVEMBER: Second Treaty of Paris.
10 DECEMBER: Napoleon moves into Longwood House.

The songs of Émile Debraux contribute to the growth of anti-Napoleonic historiography. After Waterloo, rumors of Napoleon's return to power circulate and would continue until 1821, only to be replaced by rumors denying the death of the Emperor.

1816

25 NOVEMBER: Las Cases expelled and forced to leave St. Helena. Heine publishes his anti-Napoleonic poem 'The Two Grenadiers.'

1817

Publication of the first volumes of the *Victoires et Conquêtes des Français* by Beauvais, Thiébault, and Parisot. Béranger's first song, 'La Vivandière,' inspired by the legend.
Charlet's first lithograph, entitled *Le Grenadier de Waterloo*.

1818

11 FEBRUARY: Napoleon's last interview with Gourgaud, who asked to leave St. Helena.

Béranger, 'Le Champ d'Asyle.'
Delavigne, *Les Messéniennes*, texts celebrating the glory of the French and the Grand Army.
Mme de Staël, *Considérations sur les principaux événements de la Révolution française*, a posthumous work highly critical of Napoleon

1821

5 MAY: Napoleon dies at 17:49. Several writers deal with the event, among them the Italian Manzoni in 'Il cinque Maggio' and the Austrian Grillparzer in *Napoleon*.

1822

Napoleon's silhouette and effigy begin to appear on ordinary objects.
Hugo, 'Buonaparte,' a hostile ode.
Lebrun, 'Poème lyrique sur la mort de Napoléon Ier,' a sympathetic ode..

1823

Las Cases, *Mémorial de Sainte-Hélène*. Among its mythic themes, that of Prometheus figures large. In its wake come numerous memoirs and reminiscences by major figures of the time. Among notable works of literature should be cited Pushkin's 'Ode to Napoleon' and Lamartine's 'Bonaparte.'

1827

Hugo, 'La Colonne Vendôme,' an ode that marks a decisive turning point in the relationship of Hugolian and romantic poetry to Napoleon.
Jean-Baptiste Pérès, *Comme quoi Napoléon n'a jamais existé*, the first what-if history (uchronia), already ironic.
Walter Scott, *The Life of Napoleon Bonaparte*, a biography that provokes great debate in France.

1828

Barthélemy and Méry, *Napoléon en Égypte*, the first grand work of poetic hagiography with Napoleon as superman. Later would come the authors' *Le Fils de l'homme*.

1829

Henrik Wergeland's 'Ode to Napoleon' published in Norway, one example among many reflecting the legend's broad, even world-wide diffusion.

1830
Balzac, *La Vendetta*, in which Bonaparte appears for the first time as a character in fiction. Napoleon, the memory of him, or his legend would play an important role in Balzac's *Comédie humaine* (e.g., *Le Colonel Chabert* [1832]). Throughout the year the French theatre produces play after play based upon Napoleon. Over the next ten years there would be 97 plays celebrating the fallen Emperor's *gloire*, most of them mounted in Paris.
Stendhal, *Le Rouge et le Noir*, the first great novel permeated with the legend.

1831
Alexandre Dumas's *Napoléon Bonaparte ou Trente Ans de l'histoire de France* staged in Paris, starring Frédérick Lemaître.
Auguste Barbier, 'L'Idole,' rare exemple of Romantic poetry dedicated to Napoleon at a time of anti-Bonaparte sentiment.

1832
Louis Geoffroy, *Napoléon et la conquête du monde*, the first true uchronia. A new statue is placed atop the Vendôme Column.

1833
Balzac, *Le Médecin de campagne*, which contains a chapter entitled 'Le Napoléon du peuple' ('The People's Napoleon').

1834
Sainte-Beuve, *Volupté*, which describes a military parade at the Tuileries.
Berlioz, *Le Cinq Mai ou la Mort de Napoléon*, a cantata.
Mickiewicz, *Pan Tadeusz,* which deals with the importance of Napoleon in the collective memory of Poland.

1836
Edgar Quinet, *Napoléon*, an epic.
Musset, *Les Confessions d'un enfant du siècle*, in which the author evokes the significance of Napoleon for the Romantic generation.

The Arc de Triomphe de l'Étoile is inaugurated.
In Strasbourg, Louis Napoléon Bonaparte attempts to rouse the local garrison with cries of *Vive l'Empereur!*

1839
Alexandre Dumas, *Napoléon*, an historic biography.

1840
Delaroche's painting *Napoléon at Fontainebleau.*
15 DECEMBER: The return of Napoleon's ashes to Paris.

1845
The first installment of Thiers's *L'Histoire du Consulat et de l'Empire*, one of the century's great works of history, which would continue to appear all the way to 1862.

1848
Chateaubriand, *Mémoires d'outre-tombe*, published in series and in volumes, the first of which appear during this year, the last in 1850. An important section on Napoleon.

1852
2 DECEMBER: Louis Napoléon Bonaparte, nephew of Napoleon I, is proclaimed Emperor of the French. He would reign as Napoleon III.
Karl Marx, *The 18th Brumaire of Louis Napoleon Bonaparte.*

1853
Hugo, *Les Châtiments*, a collection of poetry in which the author devalues the figure of Napoleon III in relation to that of Napoleon I. He also keeps his distance from the Napoleonic legend by showing how 18 Brumaire contained the germ of the coup d'état carried out by Louis Napoléon Bonaparte.

1860
The painter Meissonier commences work on his masterpiece, *The French Campaign, 1814.*

1862
Hugo, *Les Misérables*, a monumental

novel that includes a detailed reconstruction of the Battle of Waterloo.

1863
Erckmann-Chatrian, *Madame Thérèse*, followed by *Histoire d'un conscrit de 1813* (1864); *Waterloo* (1865); and *L'Invasion* (1867). The novels cast the Napoleonic reign in a negative light, mainly by concentrating on the lives of soldiers and ordinary people.

1868
Tolstoy, *War and Peace*, in which Napoleon is seen as the Antichrist.

1870
4 DECEMBER: France defeated in the brief Franco-Prussian War, causing the collapse of the Second Empire.

1871
The Commune topples the Vendôme Column.

1872
Napoleon indicted by Michelet in his multi-volume *Histoire du XIXᵉ siècle.*

1875
Constitution of the Third Republic.

1882
Nietzsche, *The Gay Science*, in which Napoleon is seen as a superman.

1884
Lavisse formulates a school-book version of Napoleon, condemning the despot while lauding the victorious Emperor.

1888
Taine, writing about the Empire for his six-volume *Origines de la France contemporaine*, focuses on the 'radical otherness' of Napoleon, thus providing another version of the dark legend.

1893
Frédéric Masson publishes *Napoléon et les femmes*, a work that prraises the great man.
Victorien Sardou's *Madame Sans-Gêne* makes its debut on the Paris stage.

1897
Barrès, *Les Déracinés*. Napoleon defined as professor of energy, which becomes fundamental to the Napoleonic myth under the Third Republic.

1900
Sarah Bernhardt triumphs in *L'Aiglon* (*The Eaglet*), a play about the Roi de Rome (Duke of Reichstadt) by Edmond Rostand.

1903
L'Épopée napoléonienne, the first major film produced by Pathé.

1912
Léon Bloy, *L'Âme de Napoléon*, an apotheosis of the legend and the myth. The *Revue des études napoléoniennes* founded.

1921
The bicentenary of Napoléon's death is observed. Lectures by Marshal Foch at the Invalides.
Élie Faure, *Napoléon*, the best literary example of the legend and myth published in the 20th century. Compares Napoleon to Jesus Christ.

1925
Emil Ludwig, *Napoleon*, a product of German romanticism.

1927
Napoléon vu par Abel Gance, one of the first great films on the subject.

1929
Joseph Delteil, *Il était une fois Napoléon*, a work of hagiography.
Maurras, *Napoléon avec la France ou contre la France*. Canonic interpretation of the Napoleonic era by the theoretician of the right-wing movement Action Française. In 1939 Léon Daudet would go one better with his *Deux Idoles sanguinaires: La Révolution et son fils Bonaparte*.

1930
Malraux, *Vie de Napoléon par lui-même*, a celebration of the great man, as if the author were preparing for the day when he could sing the praises of de Gaulle.

1931
Jacques Bainville, *Napoléon*, a work of critical history from a perspective close to that of Action Française.
Curzio Malaparte, *Technique du coup d'État*, a political analysis of the subject as the first modern statesman.

1932
The Institut Napoléon founded in Paris.

1935
Louis Madelin, *Napoléon*, an historical work sympathetic to its subject.

1936
Eugène Tarlé, *Napoléon*, a Marxist work from the Soviet Union.
Octave Aubry, *Napoléon*, another historical treatment sympathetic in its point of view.

1937–1954
Louis Madelin, *Histoire du Consulat et de l'Empire*, one of the century's great works of historiography.

1938
The *Revue de l'Institut Napoléon* replaces the *Revue des études napoléoniennes*.

1940
15 DECEMBER: The ashes of l'Aiglon transferred from Vienna to Paris, on orders from the Occupation government.

1955
Napoléon, a film by Sacha Guitry with Daniel Gélin as Bonaparte and Raymond Pellegrin as Napoleon.

1960
Austerlitz, a film by Abel Gance with Pierre Mondy as the Emperor.

1965
Jean Tulard, *L'Anti-Napoléon: La légende noire de l'Empereur*, the first major book on the issue in modern times.

1969
Henri Viard, *La Bande à Bonape*, a Napoleon in a series known for dark parody.

Marcel Lenormand, *Il faut fusiller Napoléon*; equates Napoleon with Hitler.
Henri Guillemin, *Napoléon tel quel*, a revival of the dark legend.
15 AUGUST: Commemoration of the bicentenary of Napoleon's birth, with a lecture by Georges Pompidou in Ajaccio.

1970
Waterloo, a film by Sergei Bondartchuk starring Rod Steiger.

1971
Albert Manfred, *Napoléon Bonaparte*, a monument of Marxist interpretation.
Jean Tulard, *Le Mythe de Napoléon*, the first major work of synthesis on the whole issue of Napoleonic myth.

1977
Jean Tulard, *Napoléon ou le Mythe du sauveur*, the work of history for our time.

1978
Sten Forshufvud and Ben Weider, *Assassination at Saint-Helena*, an exploration of the theory of Napoleon's death from poisoning, which would find a considerable following.

1986
Simon Leys, *La Mort de Napoléon*, the most delightful of the 'uchronias.'

1987
The *Dictionnaire Napoléon*, edited by Jean Tulard.

Since 1989
Innumerable publications, cinematic works, and various manifestations. Jean Dutourd revives the uchronia genre with *Le Feld-Maréchal von Bonaparte* (1996). Patrick Rambaud receives the Prix Goncourt in 1997 for *La Bataille*. The dark legend finds a new champion in Roger Caratini (*Napoléon, une imposture*, 1998). Inauguration of the bimonthly *Napoléon Ier, le magazine du Consulat et de l'Empire* (1999). The next to last 'San Antonio' is titled *Napoléon Pommier* (2000).

Bibliography

Agulhon, Maurice, *Coup d'État et République*, Paris, 1997.

—, *Histoire, symbole, mythe*, Paris, 1998.

Amalvi, Christian, *De l'art et la manière d'accommoder les héros de l'histoire de France: Essais de mythologie nationale*, Paris, 1988.

Asprey, Robert, *The Reign of Napoelon Bonaparte*, London, NY, 2002

—, *The Rise of Napoleon Bonaparte*, London, NY, 2001.

Barbier, Pierre, and France Vernillat, *Napoléon et sa légende*, vol. 5 of *L'Histoire de France par les chansons*, Paris, 1958.

Barnett, Corelli, *Bonaparte*, New York, 1978.

Bergeron, Louis, 'L'Épisode napoléonien (1799–1815): Aspects intérieurs,' *Nouvelle histoire de la France contemporaine*, vol. 4, Paris, 1972.

—, *France under Napoleon*, Princeton, 1981.

Bertaud, Jean-Paul, *Le Consulat et l'Empire, 1799–1815*, Paris, 1989.

—, *La France de Napoléon*, Paris, 1987.

Blackburn, Julia, *The Emperor's Last Island: A Journey to St. Helena*, London,1991.

Bluche, Frédéric, *Le Bonapartisme*, Paris, 1981.

Boime, Albert, *Art in the Age of Bonapartism: 1800–1815*, Chicago, 1990.

Boisson, Jean, *Le Retour des cendres*, Paris,1973.

Boudon, Jacques-Olivier, ed., *Brumaire, la prise du pouvoir de Bonaparte*, Paris, 2002.

Bowden, Scott, *Armies at Waterloo: A Detailed Analysis of the Armies that Fought History's Greatest Battle*, Arlington, Tex., 1983.

Brett-James, Antony, *The Hundred Days: Napoleon's Last Campaign from Eye-Witness Accounts*, London, 1964.

Bruce, Evangeline, *Napoleon and Josephine: An Improbable Marriage*, N.Y., 1995.

Burnand, R., and E. Boucher, *L'Histoire de Napoléon racontée par les grands écrivains*, Paris, 1921.

Cabanis, José, *Le Sacre de Napoléon*, Paris, 1970, 1994.

Centlivres, Pierre, Daniel Fabre, and Françoise Zonabend, eds., *La Fabrique des héros*, Paris, 1999.

Chandler, David G., *On the Napoleonic Wars*, London, 1994.

Chappet, Alain, Roger Martin, Alain Pigeard, and André Robe, *Répertoire mondial des souvenirs napoléoniens*, Paris, 1993.

Chassé Charles, *Napoléon par les écrivains*, Paris, 1921.

Chevallier, Bernard, ed., with photographs by Marc Walter, *Style Empire*, Paris, 2001.

—, *L'ABCdaire des châteaux de Malmaison et de Bois-Préau*, Paris, 1997.

Cronin, Vincent, *Napoleon*, London 1971.

Dechamps, Jules, *Sur la légende de Napoléon*, Paris, 1931.

Delorme, Eleanor, *Josephine: Napoleon's Incomparable Empress*, New York, 2002.

Descotes, Maurice, *La Légende de Napoléon et les écrivains français du xixe siècle*, Paris, 1967.

Doyle, William, *The Oxford History of the French Revolution*, Oxford, 1989.

Draper, J.J., *The Arts under Napoleon*, New York, 1969.

Etting, John R., *Swords around a Throne: Napoleon's Grand Army*, New York, 1988.

Fierro, Alfred, André Palluel-Guillard, and Jean Tulard, *Histoire et Dictionnaire du Consulat et de l'Empire*, Paris, 1995.

Francastel, Pierre, *Le Style Empire*, 1939.

Furet, François, *La Révolution, 1780–1880*, Paris, 1988.

Garros, Louis, and Jean Tulard, *Itinéraire de Napoléon au jour le jour*, Paris, 1992.

Gengembre, Gérard, *Napoléon*, Paris, 2001.

Geyl, Pieter, *Napoleon, For and Against*, New Haven, 1949.

Giles, Frank, *Napoleon Bonaparte: England's Prisoner: The Emperor in Exile*, Berkeley, 2002.

Girardet, Raoul, *Mythes et mythologies politiques*, Paris, 1986.

Gonnard, Philippe, *Les Origines de la légende napoléonienne*, 1906, Geneva, 1974.

Gonzalez-Palacios, Alvar, *The French Empire Style*, London, 1970.

Grandjean, Serge, *Empire Furniture 1800–1825*, London, 1970.

Guerrini, Maurice, *Napoleon and Paris*, London, 1970.

Hamilton-Williams, David, *The Fall of Napoleon: The Final Betrayal*, London, 1994.

Hibbert, Christopher, *Napoleon: His Wives and Women*, New York, 2002

Holtman, R.B., *Napoleonic Propaganda*, Baton Rouge, 1950.

Humbert, Jean-Marcel, Michael Pantazzi, and Christiane Ziegler, *Egyptomania: Egypt in Western Art: 1730–1930*, Paris and Ottowa, 1994.

Johnson, Paul, *Napoleon*, London, 2002.

Jourdan, Annie, *L'Empire de Napoléon*, Paris, 2000.

—, *Napoléon, héros, imperator, mécène*, Paris, 1998.

L'Anti-Napoléon: Caricatures et satires du Consulat à l'Empire, exh. cat., Malmaison amd Bois-Préau, Paris, 1996.

Lachouque, Henry, *Napoleon's Battles: A History of His Campaigns*, New York, 1966.

Latreille, André, *L'Ère napoléonienne*, Paris, 1974.

Lefebvre, Georges, *Napoleon*, 2 vols., London, 1969.

Lentz, Thierry, *Le 18 Brumaire: Les Coups d'État de Napoléon Bonaparte*, Paris, 1997.

—, *Le Grand Consulat*, Paris, 1999.

—, *Napoléon: Idées reçues*, Paris, 2001.

Léri, Jean-Marc, *Napoléon: Le pouvoir, la nation, la légende*, Paris, 1997.

Lovie, Jacques, and André Palluel-Guillard, 'L'Épisode napoléonien (1799–1815): Aspects extérieurs,' *Nouvelle histoire de la France contemporaine*, vol. 5, Paris, 1972.

Lovigny, Christophe, and Alain Dautriat, *Napoléon, la photobiographie*, Paris, 2000.

Lucas-Dubreton, Jean, *Le Culte de Napoléon (1815–1848)*, Paris, 1960.

Lyons, Martyn, *Napoleon Bonaparte and the Legacy of the French Revolution*, New York, 1994.

Mansel, Philip, *The Eagle in Splendour: Napoleon I and His Court*, 1987.

Markham, Felix, *Napoleon*, London, 1963.

Martineau, Gilbert, *Le Retour des Cendres*, Paris, 1990.

Mattéi, Jean-Pierre, ed., *Napoléon et le cinéma: Un siècle d'images*, Ajaccio, 1998.

McGlynn, Frank, *Napoleon: A Biography*, London, 1997.

Ménager, Bernard, *Les Napoléon du peuple*, Paris, 1988.

Miquel, Pierre, *La Campagne de France de Napoléon*, Paris, 1991.

Morton, J.B., *Brumaire: The Rise of Bonaparte*, 1976.

Mossiker, Frances, *Napoleon and Josephine*, London, 1965.

Napoléon de l'histoire à la légende, Acts of the Colloqium, 30 November–1 December, Paris, 2000.

Napoléon et la famille impériale, exh. cat., Ajaccio, July–September 1969.

Napoléon vu à travers la caricature, Lausanne, 1998.

Noirot, Paul, ed., *Napoléon Bonaparte: Comment il a enivré la littérature*, Paris, 1999.

Petiteau, Natalie, *Napoléon, de la mythologie à l'histoire*, Paris, 1999.

Riehn, Richard K., *Napoleon's Russian Campaign*, New York, 1991.

Rose, John Holland, *The Life of Napoleon I*, London, 1924.

Schlenoff, Norman, 'Baron Gros and Napoleon's Egyptian Campaign,' *Essays in Honour of Walter Friedlander*, New York, 1965.

Schom, Alan, *Napoleon Bonaparte*, New York, 1997.

Sloan, William M., *Life of Napoelon Bonaparte*.

Sutherland, D.M.G., *France 1789–1815: Revolution and Counter-Revolution*, London, 1985.

Thompson, J.M., and Norman Hampson, *Napoleon Bonaparte*, London, 2001.

Tulard, Jean, Gérard Gengembre, Adrien Goetz, Jacques Jourquin, and Thierry Lentz, *L'ABCdaire de Napoléon et l'Empire*, Paris, 1998.

Tulard Jean, *L'Anti-Napoléon: La légende noire de l'Empereur*, Paris, 1965.

—, ed., *Dictionnaire Napoléon*, Paris, 1987, 1999.

—, *Le Directoire et le Consulat*, Paris, 1991.

—, ed., *L'Europe de Napoléon*, Le Coteau, 1989.

—, *La France de la Révolution et de l'Empire*, Paris, 1995.

—, Alfred Fierro, and Jean-Marc Léri, *L'Histoire de Napoléon par la peinture*, Paris, 1991.

—, *Le Mythe de Napoléon*, Paris, 1971.

—, *Napoléon, une journée particulière: 12 octobre 1809*, Paris, 1994.

—, *Napoleon: The Myth of the Saviour*, London, 1985.

—, *Napoléon, le pouvoir, la nation, la légende*, Paris, 1997.

—, *Napoléon, le Sacre*, Paris, 1994.

—, *Le 18 Brumaire: Comment terminer une révolution*, Paris, 1999.

—, *Les Vingt Jours: Louis XVIII ou Napoléon Ier? –20 mars 1815*, Paris, 2001.

Villepin, Dominique de, *Les Cent-Jours ou l'esprit de sacrifice*, Paris, 2001.

Weider, Ben, and David Hapgood, *The Murder of Napoleon*, 1983.

Weider, Ben, and Sten Forshufvud, *Assassination at St. Helena Revisited*, 1995.

Wilson-Smith, Timothy, *Napoleon and His Artists*, London, 1996.

Woolf, Stuart, *Napoléon et la conquête de l'Europe*, Paris, 1990.

Internet sites

There are numerous websites dedicated to Napoleon. Readers interested in pursuing the Napoleonic story further should perhaps begin with the two sites maintained by the Fondation Napoléon:
www.napoleon.org
www.napoleonica.org (this one especially for documents and archives).
An excellent site in English is:
www.Napoleonbonaparte.nl.

Filmography

1897: *Entrevue de Napoléon et du Pape*, Auguste and Louis Lumière (France).

1903: *L'Épopée napoléonienne*, Lucien Nonguet (France).

1907: *Napoleon and Empress Josephine of France*, James Stuart Blackton (USA).

1907: *Napoléon*, Lucien Nonguet (France).

1907: *1814*, Louis Feuillade (France).

1910: *Napoleon in Russia*, Vassili Gontcharov (Russia).

1911: *Le Mémorial de Sainte-Hélène*, Michel Carré and Barbier (France).

1911: *Napoleone a Sant'Elena*, Mario Caserini (Italy).

1914: *Napoleone, epopea napoleonica*, Bencivega (Italy).

1914: *The Man of Destiny*, Edwin, with W. Humphrey (USA).

1914: *Napoléon, du sacre à Sainte-Hélène*, Alfred Machin, with Charlier (France).

1925: *Destinée! ou Ceux de l'an IV*, Henry Roussel, with Jean-Napoléon Michel (France).

1927: *Napoléon vu par Abel Gance*, Abel Gance, with Albert Dieudonné as Bonaparte (France).

1928: *Napoleon's Barber*, John Ford, with Otto Matiesen (USA).

1928: *Napoleon auf Sankt-Helena*, Lupu Pick, with Werner Krauss (Germany).

1929: *Waterloo*, Karl Grüne, with Charles Vanel (Germany).

1935: *Napoléon vu et entendu par Abel Gance*, Abel Gance (France).

1935: *Hundert tage*, Wenzler, with Werner Krauss (Germany).

1935: *Campo di Maggio*, Giovacchino Forzano after Mussolini, with Corrado Racca (Italy).

1937: *Conquest (Marie Walewska)*, Clarence Brown, with Charles Boyer as Napoleon and Greta Garbo in Marie (USA).

1938: *A Royal Divorce*, Jack Raymond, with Pierre Blanchar (Great Britain).

1942: *Le Destin fabuleux de Désirée Clary*, Sacha Guitry, with Jean-Louis Barrault as Bonaparte and Sacha Guitry as Napoleon (France).

1954: *Désirée*, Henry Koster, with Marlon Brando as Bonaparte and Jean Simmons in the title role (USA).

1955: *Napoléon*, Sacha Guitry, with Daniel Gélin as Bonaparte and Raymond Pellegrin as Napoleon (France).

1957: *Napoléon et Marie Walewska* (television film), Lorenzi (France).

1960: *Austerlitz*, Abel Gance (France).

1961: *Le Drame de Sainte-Hélène* (television film), Lessertisseur (France).

1970: *Waterloo*, Serguei Bondartchuk, with Rod Steiger (USSR / Italy).

1979: *Joséphine ou la Comédie des ambitions* (television film), Robert Mazoyer, with Daniel Mesguich (France).

1984: *Adieu Bonaparte*, Youssef Chahine, with Patrice Chéreau (France / Egypt).

1988: *L'Otage de l'Europe*, Jerzy Kawalerowicz, with Roland Blanche (Poland).

1989: *Napoléon et l'Europe* (television film in six episodes) with Jean-François Stévenin (international co-production).

2002: *Napoléon*, directed by Yves Simoneau, adapted by Didier Decoin from a work by Max Gallo, with Christian Clavier, Isabella Rossellini, Gérard Depardieu, and John Malkowitch. A cycle of four television films produced by Jean-Pierre Guérin—GMT Productions (a subsidiary of Lagardère Media); co-produced by France 2, KirchMedia (Germany), Transfilm (Canada), Spice Factory (UK), Mafilm ASP (Hungary), RAI (Italy), and DD Productions.

Index

Photographic credits

Emmanuel Valentin (Collection Pierre-Jean Chalençon): pp. 8, 9-13 (background), 19 below, 29, 47, 55 above, 60 left, 61, 68 above, 71 above left, 72-73, 90, 92 above right and below, 94, 103, 120-121, 122-123, 124-125, 126-127, 146-147, 173, 228-229, 230-231, 232-233, 234-235, 236-237, 238-239, 240-241, 242 above, 245. **Emmanuel Valentin (Collection Ben Weider):** pp. 242 below, 243. **Emmanuel Valentin:** pp. 198 below, 199, 215.

Marc Walter: pp. 14-15, 17, 19 below, 32-33, 40-41, 42 below, 51, 52-53, 56, 110, 116, 144 below, 212-213, 216, 217, 221 above, 222, 224 left and right, 225, 226 below, 227 below.

p. 1: RMN. p. 4: Visioars/AKG Paris. p. 6: Josse. p. 8: RMN. p. 13: Bridgeman Giraudon. p. 16: ND-Viollet. p. 18: Collection Viollet. p. 19 above: AKG Paris. p. 20: Josse. p. 21: Collection Viollet. pp. 22-23: Josse. pp. 24-25: Josse. p. 25 above: Josse. p. 25 below: Photothèque Hachette. p. 26: RMN–Gérard Blot. pp. 26-27: Josse. pp. 28-29: Josse. p. 30: Josse. p. 31: Erich Lessing/AKG Paris. pp. 34-35: Josse. p. 36: RMN–Gérard Blot. p. 37: Rue des Archives. p. 38: Bridgeman Giraudon-Lauros. p. 39: Josse. p. 42 above: Josse. p. 43: Rue des Archives. p. 44: Bridgeman Giraudon-Lauros. p. 45: RMN–Daniel Arnaudet et Gérard Blot. p. 46 above: AKG Paris. p.46 below: Visioars/AKG Paris. pp. 48-49: Josse. p. 49: RMN. p. 50: Rue des Archives. p. 54 above: Josse. p. 54 below: Collection Viollet. p. 55 below: Hurault-Viollet. pp. 56-57: Photothèque Hachette. p. 58 above: Josse. p. 58 below: RMN–Martin André. p. 59: Josse. p. 60 right: Photothèque Hachette. p. 62: Collection Roger-Viollet. p. 63: Photothèque Hachette. pp. 64-65: RMN–Hervé Lewandowski. p. 66: RMN–Gérard Blot. p. 67: RMN. p. 68 below: Photothèque Hachette. p. 69: Collection Roger-Viollet. p. 70: Josse. p. 71 right and below: Photothèque Hachette. p. 74 above: Josse. p. 74 below: Photothèque Hachette. p. 75: Josse. pp. 76-77: Josse. p. 78: Josse. p. 79: AKG Paris. p. 80 above and below: Josse. p. 81: Josse. p. 82: RMN–Daniel Arnaudet. p. 83: Josse. p. 84 above: AKG Paris. p.

84 below: RMN–Daniel Arnaudet/Jean Schormans. p. 85 below: Josse. p. 85 above: AKG Paris. pp. 86-87: RMN. p. 87: Josse. pp. 88-89: RMN–Gérard Blot. p. 91: Collection Roger-Viollet. p. 92 above and below: RMN–Gérard Blot. p. 93: Josse. p. 95 below: RMN–Gérard Blot. p. 96 left: Photothèque Hachette, right: Josse. p. 97 above: RMN–Gérard Blot, below: Josse. p. 98: RMN–Martin André. p. 99: below: Photothèque Hachette, below: Bridgeman Giraudon. p. 100: Photothèque Hachette. p. 101: Rue des Archives. p. 102: RMN–R.G. Ojeda. p. 103 above: Photothèque Hachette. p. 104: Photothèque Hachette. p. 105: RMN. pp. 106-107: AKG Paris. pp. 108-109: Bridgeman Giraudon. p. 111: Photothèque Hachette. p. 112: AKG Paris. p. 113 above: Bridgeman Giraudon. p. 113 below: Photothèque Hachette. p. 114: Erich Lessing/AKG Paris. p. 115: RMN. p. 117 above: Bridgeman Giraudon. p. 117 below: Bridgeman Giraudon (private collection). p. 118: Josse (private collection). p. 119: RMN–Gérard Blot. p. 128: Bridgeman Giraudon-Lauros. p. 129: RMN. p. 130: RMN–Martin André. p. 131: RMN–Daniel Arnaudet. p. 132: Bridgeman Giraudon-Lauros. p. 133: Bridgeman Giraudon. p. 135: Bridgeman Giraudon. p. 137: Josse. p. 138: Josse. p. 139: Josse. pp. 140-141: Harlingue-Viollet. p. 142: AKG Paris. p. 143: Josse. p. 144 above: RMN. pp. 144-145: Rue des Archives. p. 148: Photothèque Hachette. p. 149 above and below: Photothèque Hachette. p. 150 above and below: Photothèque Hachette. p. 151: RMN-Daniel Arnaudet. p. 152 left and right: Photothèque Hachette. p. 153: Photothèque Hachette. p. 154 above: AKG Photo. p. 154 below: Photothèque Hachette. p. 155: Collection Viollet. p. 156: Bridgeman Giraudon Charmet. p. 157 above and below: Photothèque Hachette. p. 158: Bridgeman Giraudon-Lauros. p. 159: AKG Paris. p. 160: Photothèque Hachette. p. 161 above: Bridgeman Giraudon-Lauros. p. 161 below: Photothèque Hachette. p. 162 above: Photothèque Hachette. p. 162 below: AKG Paris. p. 163: left and right: Photothèque Hachette. p. 164 above and below: Photothèque Hachette. p. 165: Bridgeman Giraudon-Lauros. p. 166: RMN–J.G. Berizzi. p. 167: RMN–R.G. Ojeda. p. 169: Roger-Viollet. p. 170: Josse. p. 171: Josse.

p. 172: ND-Viollet. p. 174: AKG Paris. p. 175: AKG Paris. p. 176: Collection Viollet. p. 177 left: Collection Roger-Viollet. p. 177 right: Harlingue-Viollet. p. 178: Rue des Archives/BCA. p. 180: Collection Viollet. p. 181: Bridgeman Giraudon (private collection). pp. 182-183: Rue des Archives/CSFF. p. 184: Rue des Archives (private collection). p. 185: Landi. p. 186: Bridgeman Giraudon (Phillips, The International Fine Art Auctioneers). p. 187 right: Bridgeman Giraudon (private collection). p. 187 left: Collection Kharbine-Tapabor/ADAGP. p. 188: Lipnitzki/Roger-Viollet. p. 189 above left, above right and below right: Association La Corse et le Cinéma. p. 189 below left: René Ferracci. p. 190: Rue des Archives/AGIP. p. 191 above and below: Rue des Archives/ CSFF. p. 192 left: Association La Corse et le Cinéma. p. 192 right: Service des Archives du Film–CNC. p. 193: Rue des Archives/CSFF. p. 194 above left and above right: Association La Corse et le Cinéma. p. 194 below: Rue des Archives/CSFF. p. 195 above: Rue des Archives/BCA. p. 195 below: Cinémathèque Gaumont. p. 196 above and below: Arnaud Borrel/GMT Productions. pp. 196-197: Arnaud Borrel/GMT Productions. p. 198 above: AFP/EPA–Evgeny Dudin. p. 200 left: Rue des Archives/Varma. p. 200 right: Collection Viollet. p. 201 above left and below right: Collection Viollet. p. 201 above right: Rue des Archives/Varma. p. 202 above and below: Collection Kharbine-Tapabor/D.R. p. 203 above and below: Collection Kharbine-Tapabor/D.R. p. 204: AKG Paris. p. 205: Photothèque Hachette. p. 206 above: Collection Kharbine-Tapabor/ADAGP. p. 206 below: Collection Kharbine-Tapabor/D.R. pp. 206-207: AKG Paris. p. 208: Collection Kharbine-Tapabor/D.R. p. 209 above: Collections Banque de France. p. 209 below left and below rights: Paris, Musée de la Poste. p. 210: Photothèque Hachette. p. 211 left: Roger-Viollet. p. 211 right: Photothèque Hachette. p. 212: Photothèque Hachette. p. 214: Roger-Viollet. p. 218: RMN–Lagiewski. p. 219: RMN–Lagiewski. p. 220: RMN–Lagiewski. p. 221 below: RMN–Gérard Blot. p. 223 above: Bridgeman Giraudon. p. 223 below: RMN–Daniel Arnaudet. p. 226 above: Collection Roger-Viollet. p. 227: above: Josse.

The photographer Emmanuel Valentin thanks Ben Weider,
the *mairie* of Vallauris-Golfe Juan, and Jean-Louis Tremblais.

Editor of the French edition: Nathalie Bailleux
Design and layout: Marc Walter / Chine
Illustrations editor: David Chanteranne
Advisor on collections and sales: Pierre-Jean Chalençon

Photoengraving: Chine
Printed in Italy at Editoriale Lloyd